The

Art
of
MODERN
SALES
MANAGEMENT

Driving Performance in a Connected World

ASTD
PRESS

ASTD Press is an internationally renowned source of insightful and practical information on workplace learning, training, and professional development.

ASTD Press
1640 King Street Box 1443
Alexandria, VA 22313-1443 USA

Ordering information: Books published by ASTD Press can be purchased by visiting ASTD's website at store.astd.org or by calling 800.628.2783 or 703.683.8100.

Library of Congress Control Number: 2013957751
ISBN-10: 1-56286-897-7
ISBN-13: 978-1-56286-897-0
e-ISBN: 978-1-60728-397-3

ASTD Press Editorial Staff:
Director: Glenn Saltzman
Manager, ASTD Press: Ashley McDonald
Community of Practice Manager, Sales Enablement: Roxy Torres
Associate Editor: Sarah Cough
Editorial Assistant: Ashley Slade
Cover Design: Marisa Kelly
Interior Layout: Bey Bello, Jane deBruijn, & Lon Levy

Printed by The PA Hutchison Company, Mayfield, PA, www.pahutch.com

Contents

Introduction... v

Chapter 1: Producing Performance–*Terrence Donahue*.. 1

Chapter 2: Coaching for Performance–*Leonard Cochran*................................. 17

Chapter 3: Improving the Sales Call–*Leo Tilley*... 33

Chapter 4: Managing the Sales Team Pipeline–*Steve Gielda* 51

Chapter 5: Selling Across Cultures–*Anup Soans and Joshua Soans*................. 65

Chapter 6: Managing Global Sales Teams–*Claude Chadillon*........................... 75

Chapter 7: The Sales Manager's Role in Training–*Sandy Stricker* 89

Chapter 8: Leveraging Your EQ for Sales Effectiveness–*Lou Russell* 101

Chapter 9: The Hiring Dilemma: Advice for Sales Leaders–*Joseph Anzalone*.. 121

Chapter 10: Strategic Storytelling for Sales Managers–*Alfredo Castro*........... 137

Chapter 11: Social Media Marketing For Sales Managers–*Glenn Raines*....... 155

Chapter 12: Successfully Leading Virtual Teams–*Renie McClay* 177

Appendix: Sales Manager Skills Assessment–*Ken Phillips* 191

Introduction

We set out to develop a resource for sales management effectiveness! I hope you find this team has done just that. I expect that for every sales leader there will be topics here that you are particularly attracted to. No need to read this book cover to cover. Grab the topics that interest you the most.

I see the world through a sales lens. There are two types of company employees: those who generate revenue and those who support revenue generation. Sales and sales management are clearly the revenue-generating function of the company. On the following page is the Selling System from *World Class Selling: New Sales Competencies*; it illustrates the roles and responsibilities of those who are directly and indirectly responsible for revenue generation.

Sales managers spend their time teaching the sales team to consistently produce profitable revenue and growth to fuel the organization. As such, they must be experts on products, the industry, sales information systems, customers and prospects, internal marketing, policies and procedures, and about a dozen other topics. They also take the heat from above—managing quotas, revenue, and profitability every week of their lives. In addition, sales managers deal with the frustration on both sides of the front line—the salespeople and the savvy customers—when things are not going smoothly. Sales management, specifically sales managers, are often the unsung heroes—and the hearts–of most organizations.

I also see that the sales landscape has changed dramatically in the recent past. The sales profession has abandoned the "good old boy networks" and relying on influence and persuasion. Buyers can easily spot rehearsed sales tactics where "when they say this, you say that" to talk them into the product. They are quick to show those individuals the door. Solutions are often unique, rather than one-size-fits-many. Today's successful sales efforts require a vast and dynamic skill set to create a strategic approach to solve a business problem.

Figure 1

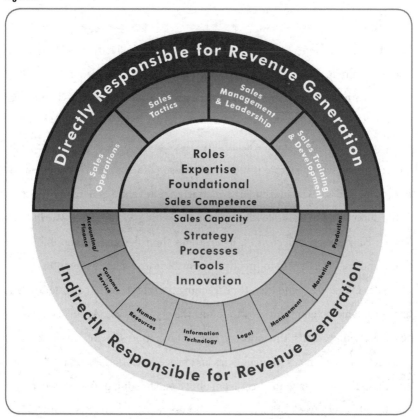

My purpose for creating this book is to help today's sales managers by preparing them for modern day sales efforts. I will do this by plugging into today's successful sales development professionals who have towering strengths and are willing to share what they know, and then translating that knowledge into actionable steps for sales managers to begin learning and mastering this new art.

Effective learning begins with an understanding of the root causes. In this case, what has led to the need for a more "modern" approach to managing sales?

Buyers are more connected and better skilled than ever before. Some large companies rotate buyers to different positions to reduce the personal relationships and loyalty to companies that can result in long-term business relationships. In turn, sales teams need to be more connected and find customers and prospects where they live, where they read, and where they search for information.

Years ago if a customer had a bad experience, it was bad for business. The company lost that revenue and it was a sad month—perhaps even a few sad years. Word may have gotten out to other local customers, but not much further. Today experiences (good and bad) can be shared very easily with critical target groups and others across the globe with a few keystrokes. Social media has changed the landscape of customer satisfaction. This new technology also creates new avenues for salespeople to find prospects and to be identified as subject matter experts and thought leaders.

We need to adapt our skill set to catch up to the buyers. We need to be more equipped to help them identify and clarify problems and establish strategic solutions. The role of sales managers in this situation is to help sales teams know how to ask the right questions and how to show that their solution can add value.

We can't just rely on "send them to training." What is more important than upskilling the sales team? Simply sending team members to training is no longer a solution for a complex problem. Who is in the best position to upskill the sales team? You guessed it, the sales manager. With the current and changing requirement of management roles, this task is often put on the back burner because of competing priorities. The manager needs to drive the development of their team through coaching, removing barriers, and enabling team collaboration. And when salespeople do attend training, they need to help maximize the time and money spent with on-the-job application and feedback.

Our intention (mine and the contributors to this book) is to enable sales management to upskill their salespeople in the areas of: improving sales performance, strengthening pipeline management, managing and selling globally, doing more informed hiring, making an impact developing salespeople, and managing the fires, while keeping relationships intact.

We've done this by designing each chapter to be actionable. Each topic provides the knowledge and information necessary to upgrade skills and make an immediate impact, in a changing landscape.

The contributors to this book are professionals who have influenced and improved sales in the companies they have worked. They have more than 180 collective years of experience developing salespeople. It has been an honor and a pleasure to work with them and to see their enthusiasm for sharing what they know with you. Our hope is that you find and use some actionable nuggets to develop a strong sales team in this modern sales landscape.

Cheers,

Renie

1

Producing Performance

Terrence Donahue

What do you produce as a sales manager?

In the several years I've been asking this question of sales managers, I've discovered it's something they've either never been asked before or never considered. It's important to take the time to consider your response. Everyone who works produces something. As a sales manager, what do you produce? I'm not asking, "What product do you sell?" or "What do you do?" My question is, "In your role as a sales manager, what do you really produce?" That's a very different question.

Consider this: Your product in your role as a sales manager is the job performance of your sales team. You are a performance maker. The most important question you will ever ask in your role is: "What must I do to create the kind of performance I need from my sales team to get the business outcomes we want?"

Asking that question takes a lot more thought than simply asking, "How do we hit our sales numbers?" And while our success as sales managers is primarily measured by our ability to deliver sales results, we will concern ourselves in this chapter with how to produce the performance that delivers those results.

Great sales managers, like great leaders, always begin with the end in mind. Follow this line of thinking as you plan your work, develop your team, and execute your strategic and tactical plans:

- What are the business outcomes I want?
- What kind of performance do I need from my sales team to get these outcomes?
- What must I do to create, drive, and sustain this kind of performance from my team to get these outcomes?

The Job Performance Equation

There are two things that both you and your sales employees should have a clear view of: What you expect of your employees and how they are performing. Here's a simple formula to explain the job performance equation.

Expected Performance – Actual Performance = Performance Discrepancy

In other words, if your sales employees aren't doing what they should be doing, there is a discrepancy in their performance. We need to know what should be happening and what is happening. Your role as a performance maker is to:

- Determine the expected performance of your sales employees.
- Measure the actual performance of your sales employees.
- Identify any discrepancies in the performance of your sales employees.
- Identify the cause(s) of any discrepancies.
- Implement the appropriate solutions to eliminate performance discrepancies.

Identifying Required Performance

The place to start in creating performance is identifying what expected (or required) performance should look like. Think beyond just hitting the sales goal. While it is important to think of the end, it is equally important to consider the best means to the end.

When I ask sales employees to describe what they should be doing in the performance of their role, most reply by telling me what they *are* doing. But what employees *should* be doing and what they *are* doing may not necessarily be the same thing.

When I ask sales managers what their sales employees should be doing, most of them reply "they should be selling more product." Very few sales managers, however, can articulate the specific activities that their sales employees should be performing in order to sell more. In other words, sales managers have not carefully thought through the means to their end. This is where the concept of a job inventory is especially helpful.

The Value of a Job Inventory

A job inventory is the most objective way of identifying the performance requirements of a sales position. A job inventory is simply a list of the tasks that a sales employee performs. It's a great precursor to a job description. Like an inventory, it takes stock of what you have compared to what you need.

There is an example of a job inventory for a distributor sales representative on the next page. In this example, the "duties" are the general areas of responsibility arising for the role, and the specific tasks related to those duties are grouped accordingly. Those are the main things called out in a job description. Each duty has associated tasks. These tasks, in terms of when they are performed, why they are performed, and how they are performed, all contribute to the job of selling.

You'll notice that all these tasks are written in the same grammatical format. They begin with an action verb followed by a noun. A sales job, like any other job, is a compilation of tasks someone must perform to fulfill the strategic purpose of that job. The strategic purpose of a sales-related job is to sell a product or service or solution to a buyer. There are a number of specific tasks involved in doing that.

Table 1.1
Job Inventory Example: Distributor Sales Representative

Duties	Tasks
Sales	Deliver assigned target account quota. Increase gross trading margin. Increase market penetration. Develop a target account list. Conduct monthly calls on target accounts. Develop distributor business plans. Conduct product demonstrations. Communicate product features and benefits. Identify customer needs. Identify competitive threats. Provide end-user solutions. Manage service activity. Close end-user sales with manufacturer.
Administration	Capture sales activities with reporting software. Complete monthly sales rep report. Read and respond to email. Check and respond to voicemail. Submit monthly expense reports. Perform sales forecast report. Maintain company vehicle. Update personal business plan. Submit rebates. Gather competitive intelligence.
Manufacturer Relationships	Work with manufacturer's rep according to schedule. Participate in sales meetings. Respond to requests. Develop strategic business plan. Conduct new product introductions. Train end-users on products and procedures. Communicate sales wins.

Depending on your company, the duties may change as the strategic drivers change. Below is an example of a job inventory for a sales operations manager. Instead of listing the traditional sales duties, the key strategic drivers are identified. The specific tasks that fall under achieving that strategic driver are grouped together accordingly.

Table 1.2
Job Inventory Example: Operations Sales Manager

Strategic Drivers	Tasks
Driving Sales	Establish KPIs for account teams. Create and deliver assigned sales budgets. Conduct team sales meetings. Identify customer needs and adapt tactical plan. Identify sales, pricing, and package opportunities. Review sales forecasts and budgets. Update planning tool weekly and assign targets with sales managers. Analyze weekly sales data and create action plans. Champion new product introductions. Track demographics and adjust tactics to drive sales.
Operational Excellence	Communicate problems and client requests to relevant sales managers. Create annual business plan. Create weekly tactical plans. Identify training needs for employees. Create performance development plans for employees. Identify best practices and benchmarks. Plan projects. Communicate changes and develop succession planning. Resolve conflicts. Present weekly sales reports to VP. Analyze sales and revenue streams. Make recommendations. Give feedback to sales employees.
Cost Containment	Identify operational inefficiencies. Eliminate inefficiencies. Monitor retail and material write-offs. Retain staff to reduce transfer costs. Forecast sales staffing. Enforce equipment policy to prevent breakage and loss. Comply with safety standards. Collaborate on budgets for new accounts.

A job inventory should always be the basis for creating a job description. After discussing and demonstrating examples of sales employee job inventories, the president of sales from one company lamented to me, "We just spent $10,000 on a consultant to write new job descriptions for our salesforces. Now after understanding how important a job inventory is to really nail down the specific requirements for a job, I realize that our new job descriptions are basically worthless."

Identifying the Actual Performance of Your Sales Employees

Once you know what your sales employees are supposed to be doing (expected performance), the next thing you need to do is determine if they are doing what they are supposed to be doing (actual performance).

Most successful sales managers do this by observing the performance of their employees during ride-alongs. While observation is a great method, employees typically perform at their best when their boss is watching.

Benchmark Where and How Your Sales Team Spends Their Time and Effort

I was once the North American director of training at a large manufacturer of cleaning chemicals made and sold for institutional markets—healthcare, food service, hospitality, and building services. While our products were well-recognized and seen as the best-performing product in the industry, we were also the premium-priced product, in a heavily commoditized market. While our distributors loved to lead with our product, many of them also carried our competitors' product in their warehouses. In a time of economic constraint and restraint, we had to create a strategy of selling value over price. Along with that, we began to wonder how similar salesforces in similar business models were doing. We launched a comprehensive benchmark with world-class salesforces that identified how we compared to others. We were quite surprised by what we found.

Administrative Tasks

Our benchmark study revealed that our sales employees were spending between 15 and 40 percent of their time on administrative tasks (expense reporting, making marketing slides, and customizing sales sheets). Our average time spent was 24 percent. World-class salesforces ranged between 9 and 17 percent of their time spent on administrative tasks. As one of our regional VP of sales put it, "driving a desk will not drive sales."

Personal Development

World-class salesforces spent 5 percent of their time on personal development, such as training, skill seminars, and webinars. Our salesforces averaged 1 percent. There was no professional development plan in place for anyone in the salesforce. Any training that took place only focused on new product launches.

Business Development and Planning

The real shock for us came when we discovered how poorly our salesforce was doing in planning their accounts. Being the premium product on the market and also having the most well-known name in the market, our salesforces would lean heavily on brand recognition rather than planning a detailed strategy with their distributors. Our salesforce averaged 4 percent of their time on business planning. World-class salesforces averaged 33 to 42 percent of their time in business planning. This was our big gap. It all came down to the old saying: "If you fail to plan, you plan to fail." This benchmarking study resulted in creating a massive salesforce effectiveness initiative across our business platforms and our nine brands. A very strict account planning process was put in place as well as accountability and measurements behind these new standards. The results we delivered from this new discipline were impressive and really changed our relationship with our distributors in a positive way.

Selling

We also discovered that our salesforce was only spending 27 percent of their time actually selling. World-class salesforces spent 27 to 40 percent of their time selling. All the other tasks around the sale were competing with making the sale. Our profit margins and brand power were carrying us for a long time. But when it comes down to it, when you are a salesperson and spending only about a quarter of your work time selling, are all the other things you're doing really driving value to deliver the results?

In summary, compared to world-class salesforces, we were spending far too much time on tasks that were not related to creating business value. We would have never known this without making the investment in a benchmarking study. It showed us where we were at compared to where we needed to be.

Benchmark High-Performing Salespeople in Your Company

A vice president of sales once approached me with a request for a major training initiative. None of the VPs could articulate exactly what the outcomes for the training should be, but all agreed that everyone in our salesforce should "sell like Gordon sells." Gordon was a top performing salesperson in the Toronto area. He constantly outperformed everyone and easily reached his stretch goals. Gordon never missed a bonus. When it all came down to it, the VPs of sales determined that they needed training "to make everyone into a Gordon." Cloning takes time, even when you are designing training. I began to look closely at Gordon and what he did, when he did it, why he did it, and how he did it and saw distinct action patterns that separated him from the rest of the pack.

I've seen this in many other sales organizations. Sales managers ask me to help "make all my sales employees as good as my best sales employee," but beyond that, they say little else. When I've asked sales managers what separates the best from the rest, about half of them just say, "Well, they are my star players, my dream salespeople."

Figure 1.1

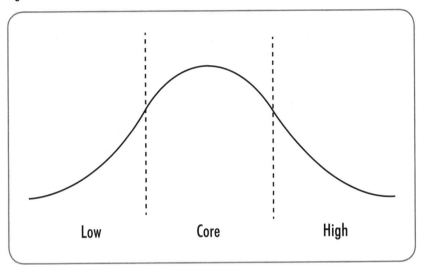

By looking at the high performers within a sales team, you can begin to identify the specific tasks they are performing and how they are doing them. You will also identify how they prioritize their tasks in such a way that it produces their high performance. This might identify possible training or developmental needs within the low performer and core performer groups as a way of bringing up the performance of the entire group.

Identify Any Performance Discrepancies

If there is a discrepancy between expected performance and actual performance, then you as the sales manager must analyze the performance discrepancy. There are three steps to follow when doing this. The first two steps focus on the problem and the cause, and the last step focuses on implementing the right solution to the problem.

Key Questions

- What are the specific tasks that the high performers are doing differently from the core and low performers?

- How are they performing those tasks differently?

- Where are the high-performing salespeople focusing their time and efforts?

- How can we "move the middle" of the performance bell curve?

- Is training a viable strategy?

- Besides training, what else needs to be in place to improve performance?

Step One: Identify the Performance Discrepancy

Once you've reviewed the data on what employees are supposed to be doing (expected performance) and on what they're really doing (actual performance), you must identify the specific required task(s) not being performed properly. In this first step it is critical to focus only on defining the job performance discrepancy (or gap), not the cause of the problem or the solutions to fix the problem.

Step Two: Identify the Cause of the Performance Discrepancy

Poor job performance always has a reason. Seven things must be in place in the work environment for employees to perform as they are required. If one or more of these seven factors of job performance is missing or deficient, there will be a gap in performance. You'll need to look at each gap in their performance and determine: What is the cause of this specific performance discrepancy?

The Seven Factors of Job Performance

Anytime you find a performance discrepancy, the cause is going to be one or more of the following seven factors of job performance.

Figure 1.2

Capacity

If the employee does not have the capacity to perform as required by the job it could cause performance discrepancy. By capacity, we are referring to physical capacity, emotional capacity, interpersonal capacity, analytical capacity, and so on. Capacity means inherent ability or talent. It's about how a person is wired.

Conditions

Another cause of performance discrepancy is if the employees lack the conditions to perform as required by the job. By conditions, we might include time, tools, information, equipment, budget, and so on. Sometimes we refer to conditions as environment.

Motivation

One reason an employee might not perform as she should is that there is not an incentive or motivation for her to perform. Incentives are a strong motivating factor for most sales employees. But sometimes, high performers are not incentivized in the right way. One example is that sometimes high performers get more work, while the low performers get less work, because the high performers will do it for them.

Knowledge and Skill

Another cause for a performance discrepancy is that employees lack the knowledge and skill to perform as needed. Anytime you find a job performance gap caused by a lack of knowledge and skill, then you know that training is an appropriate solution.

Standards

It has been my experience that the most common cause of a performance discrepancy is that the employees do not understand what required performance looks like. While they can understand the concept of "hitting your numbers" many are unclear about the specific tasks they should be performing in order to hit their numbers.

Measurement

A successful sales manager goes beyond just measuring the numbers. They pay attention to all the tasks related to making the sale, and put measurements that matter behind them.

Feedback

Successful sales managers give regular, detailed, and systematic feedback to their sales employees. Ineffective sales managers have a common method of operating when it comes to giving feedback. Their approach is "assume you're doing just fine unless I tell you otherwise." Feedback serves two purposes. It maintains good performance, and it modifies poor performance. Concern yourself just as much with maintenance feedback as you do modifying feedback.

Table 1.3

Cause	Solution
Capacity	Change personnel. Rotate responsibilities. Revise hiring practices to land more highly qualified candidates.
Conditions	Reorganize the work schedule. Upgrade materials, equipment, and information. Simplify the job. Remove or reduce distractions. Conduct a "conditions study."
Knowledge and Skill	Improve current training. Provide better reinforcement after training. Provide coaching. Provide job aids.
Incentives and Motivation	Provide or strengthen positive consequences. Review and revise existing rewards systems. Create recognition events. Establish accountabilities.
Standards	Develop job performance standards. Revise or update old standards. Clarify and confirm understanding of standards with your employees.
Measurement	Develop measurements. Revise old measurements. Ensure measurements are based on defined standards.
Feedback	Provide feedback. Improve delivery of feedback. Increase frequency of feedback.

Step Three: Implement Solutions

Once you have determined the performance discrepancy (step 1) and its cause(s) (step 2), your next action is to propose the right solution to eliminate the discrepancy. Use the tool provided to help match the right solution to the specific cause of the performance problem.

Summing It Up

In summary, the main purpose of the role of sales manager is to ensure that the sales employees are performing as expected. That's easier said than done. To recap, here's what great sales managers do:

- Determine expected performance.
- Determine actual performance.
- Identify any job performance discrepancies.
- Identify the cause of performance discrepancies.
- Implement solutions to eliminate performance discrepancies.

I'd like you to leave this chapter asking that all-important question one more time: "As a sales manager, what must I do to create the kind of performance I need from my sales team to get the business outcomes I want?"

Remember: Your product is your team's performance. You are a perfomance-maker. I hope you will never look at your job quite the same way again.

Action Plan

If I asked your sales team to describe what expected performance is for them, how accurately would they be able to articulate your expectations of them beyond the vague reference of "hitting my numbers?"

Take 20 minutes and create a simple job inventory for all the members of your sales team.

Questions for reflection:

- What is your true product as a sales manager?
- Do you consider yourself more of a supervisor or a super worker? Which one does your team need?

About the Author

Terrence Donahue built his career by providing training and performance consulting services to learning and development professionals working in the biggest names across many industries, including the Coca-Cola Company, Nike Europe, Chick-fil-A, Citibank Europe, Scandinavian Airlines, Abbott Laboratories, and the OSHA National Training Institute. Over the last 18 years he has personally trained and equipped more than 30,000 learning professionals on three continents. He has used his training and business skills to help drive major corporate initiatives in areas such as outcomes-based training, succession planning, leadership development, salesforce excellence, price increase strategies, and learning transfer. Terrence has driven results for the organizations he has worked for by introducing world-class practices and making them common practice in his organizations. He has held both strategic and tactical roles ranging from senior vice president of training and development at the world's largest training workshop provider, director of training of North America at JohnsonDiversey, and vice president of instructor quality at the National Restaurant Association. He is currently corporate director of training for Emerson Electric.

2
Coaching for Performance

Leonard Cochran

Over the course of more than 15 years managing teams from 2 to 65 people, no one has ever provided me with training on "how to coach team members." I had to learn from trial and error. In the following pages, I will share a few keys that have made my job of leading a team a lot easier. I trust you will find these helpful as well.

Let's define two terms before we begin. It's important to understand the difference between "coaching" and "feedback." In the workforce today, most people view coaching as a form of discipline. Many believe that a coaching session only occurs as a reprimand for poor performance or behavior. It's unfortunate that this has become the norm. As a former athlete in school, I would have quit the team if my coach only pulled me aside to tell me what I did wrong and warn me that I needed to improve my performance or I would be looking for another sport to play. Can you imagine that? That's crazy; no coach would ever treat his team members that way.

What Is Coaching?

Merriam-Webster defines a coach as "one who instructs or trains <an acting coach>; especially: one who instructs players in the fundamentals of a sport and directs team strategy."

When ASTD presented the new Competency Model in the January 2013 issue of *T+D*, they defined coaching as: "Using an interactive process to help individuals develop rapidly and produce results; improving others' ability to set goals, take action, make better decisions, and make full use of their natural strengths." So, coaching someone or a team simply means providing instruction and support for the team to be as successful as they can.

Merriam-Webster defines feedback as: "the transmission of evaluative or corrective information about an action, event, or process to the original or controlling source."

Do you notice how neither coaching nor feedback has a negative connotation by definition? I'm guessing the negative association comes from the fact that most of us are only evaluated annually. Sometimes that's the only time we receive feedback or coaching, and then it's given to justify why we received (or did not receive) an annual increase.

No winning coach rests on their wins from last season. Every coach recognizes there is always opportunity for growth and development. Properly coaching a sales team will help your team align their individual goals with the goals of the business and create a "winning" team.

There are two primary areas of focus that we need to look at when working with a team. We will start by focusing on the team members, and then we will focus on the skills of the team leader.

Focus on the Team: Set Up the Team for Success

As a coach, you are only as successful as your team, so it's important to set up your team for success. Here are the key questions that can help ensure that you have done just that.

Has Proper Training Been Provided to Each Member on the Team?

It's amazing how important it is to train our team members, yet we seldom have the time or budget to train them properly. Training provides the foundation for baseline skills in which you will coach your sales team. I heard Zig Ziglar speak once and a story he shared summarized it best. It went something like this: "When you raise children, it's going to cost you. You have got to invest in them. You have got to invest your time in them. If you invest your time in them when they are young, they'll be a blessing to you when they are older. If you don't spend time with your children when they're young, you'll spend your time on them when they are older—you'll spend your time talking to their teachers about why they're doing poorly in school, or you'll spend your time bailing them out of trouble." When we manage a sales team, the "pay now or pay later" principle is also true. We can spend time training our team members correctly when they are first hired or we can spend our time trying to fix issues later. Proper training and coaching can prevent this trouble. Either way, it's going to cost you, so decide if you want to pay now or pay later. My advice is to make the investment early.

As part of training, it's great for team members to learn from other team members, but it's also important that they learn from you, their manager. It demonstrates the importance you place on sales training. It also demonstrates the value you place on them since you're investing your time in them. Ask yourself the following questions:

- Do new sales team members know the sales process for your company?

- Do they know and understand how commissions and bonus programs work?

- Do they know:
  - the company
  - the competition
  - where to get answers to their questions
  - what paperwork is required and how to do it?

- What training are you providing for existing team members?

- Do they know:
  - current industry and/or market trends
  - new tools available to perform their jobs
  - how to effectively prospect using the Internet?

- Are there leadership skills they should learn to help strengthen the team?

Take Bill for example. Bill was an outstanding salesman but he was never very good at keeping up with his paperwork. On several occasions I complimented him on his selling skills while subtlety reminding him of the importance of doing his paperwork. One day Bill brought in an order for the largest single purchase by a client. Everyone in the office was thrilled. When it came time for delivery, the customer only accepted half of the order. When I went to review the contract, I found that Bill had failed to get the customer's signature on the paperwork. So, we were left trying to figure out how to move the second half of the order. Had I coached Bill on the importance of the process and held him accountable for his paperwork, this whole issue could have been avoided, but I was too afraid of upsetting my best salesman. I had failed him, and in turn, he failed me.

As the sales manager, share your knowledge. Several studies show that up to 70 percent of our learning comes informally. Use short team meetings as an opportunity to update the team on current trends and for short teachable coaching moments. Allow team members to share best practices or to share in areas that they excel. This can help to create a collaborative environment, even in a competitive sales team!

Proper sales training is also a great way to help you retain talent. It used to be that people would fear training employees "up and out." There used to be a mindset that if employees increased their knowledge on the job, they might leave one company to get a promotion at another. This was a particularly common mindset in the sales profession. In the work environment today, this is no longer true (if it ever was). Most people realize that the more knowledge they gain, the more value they bring to the team. Often the more value they bring to the team, the more loyal they become to the company they work for. And, does a sales leader really want to retain untrained salespeople?

Have Clear Expectations Been Set?

Somehow we always think we are clear in our communication and yet we're often misunderstood. Have you set clear expectations for your team? Do they have clear sales goals? Are there standards they should be following? Are there deadlines that must be met? If you haven't told them what the expectations are, how can you expect them to know the answer to these questions?

If you need guidance on how to best communicate expectations to your team, you may be interested in reading Dr. Paul Hersey's book *The Situational Leader*. He provides insight into how to communicate with team members based on the development level of the person that you're working with. Ken Blanchard has an excellent program based on this theory, which is available through his organization. In short, not everyone on your team needs to have the exact same expectations, because they should be determined on the basis of each team member's ability and experience. No one would expect someone in their first year of sales to have the same sales goals as a veteran salesperson.

Be sure to set SMART objectives and SMART goals when possible. SMART is an acronym that stands for: specific, measurable, achievable, realistic, and time-bound. If you are not familiar with SMART goals, do a quick search on the Internet and read up on it. It's a great model to help you set clear goals and expectations. Allow each team member to contribute to their own SMART goals. People tend to be more committed to achieving goals when they set their own (or at least contribute to making their own goals).

Has Enough Time for Mastery Been Provided?

Once your team is properly trained, and they have a clear understanding of their expectations, it's important to allow enough time for team members to master the skills to perform their duties to their full potential. As you coach your sales team, it's important to remember not everyone learns at the same speed, just as everyone does not reach top-level performance at the same speed. In this day and age, we cannot afford to have someone not prepared and performing quickly. At the same time, we cannot afford to be too hasty in getting them up to speed, or we may find they never master the skills needed to be successful in their position.

Setting goals just beyond the comfort zone of the team members is a great way to help people grow their skills. "Stretch goals" are a healthy way to help team members gain mastery without overwhelming them. It allows them enough time to master their skills at a comfortable pace.

There is an additional consideration when looking for someone to master a skill: Does she want to master the required skill? Some years ago I had an employee that had been trained and had adequate enough time to master her duties, yet she just never seemed to take ownership of responsibilities. Let's call her Sue. Sue did an average job, and I had the feeling that she wasn't trying. One day at work Bob was absent and Sue had to take his place. She had to perform duties, that she hadn't done before because no one else was available. To my surprise, Sue caught on quickly and performed the job extremely well. When I complimented her skills, she politely informed me that she would like to help Bob all the time because she didn't enjoy the work she had been doing. I learned an important lesson that day about job mastery; take the time to determine if you have the right person in the right position.

The Importance of Consistency

- Am I consistent in expectations?
- Am I consistent in communication?
- Am I consistent in discipline?

Focus on the Team Leader: The Importance of Consistency

I have discovered that much of the weight of a great team's performance falls on the leadership of the team. There have been athletes with great abilities that have played on teams with other great athletes and they did not perform well as a team. Yet, there have also been average teams that have had great coaching, and they have performed beyond anyone's expectations. Let's take a moment to focus on the importance of the team leader in a sales team.

Am I Consistent in Expectations?

Being consistent brings a sense of security to the team. I've often said that even a bad manager, if he is consistent, is better than a good manager who is inconsistent. Why? Because you can learn to work around someone who is consistently bad, but when someone is inconsistent, you never know what to expect.

Being consistent in your expectations helps to ensure the consistency of your team's performance—provided you are following up with them. You have likely heard the saying "you get what you inspect, not what you expect." That's a simple statement to remind us to be consistent in our follow up.

To be consistent, you have to be deliberate. Put a reminder on your calendar until it becomes a natural habit for you. Is the annual employee evaluation the only time that you talk to your team members about their performance? Instead, schedule time to talk to your team members one-on-one on a monthly or even weekly basis. Talk about their performance; regularly provide both feedback and coaching to individuals. Share what they are doing right, and provide guidance on how they can do better. What sports team has a coach that only talks to them once a year and tells them how they're doing? Not one! The coach is consistently there with the team on a daily basis guiding them and encouraging them!

Am I Consistent in Communication?

Do you have weekly or monthly meetings with your team to provide everyone an opportunity to "check in"? Communication is a vital part of any successful team. How can we expect our teams to perform if there is little or no communication? Provide the time and opportunity for everyone to be heard and to provide feedback on what is important to them. As the sales manager, you should be setting the example in communication. Open, honest communication will help your team feel valued and respected. And don't forget the value of saying "thank you"—if your team members have earned your appreciation, they should hear it from you.

As I said earlier, consistency may require you to put the time on your calendar until it becomes a natural part of your day. Determine what method of communication is most appropriate for your team (phone call, email, or face-to-face meetings) and then do it! Keep in mind communication is an exchange of information. Allow others an opportunity to respond or to share.

Don't do all the talking yourself. Is there a team member that has an area of expertise that he can share with the team? Make that a part of your regular routine. Spotlight others and watch them shine.

Am I Consistent in Discipline?

No one likes administering discipline. No one. Yet, discipline is necessary to help people grow. As the disciplinarian, you will need to be a person of your word. There is nothing that will strip you of your power quicker than spouting out threats that are never followed up on. That behavior conditions people to believe that you are not serious about what you are threatening. Say what you mean, and mean what you say.

In addition, you have to lead by example. Your team will be watching you and monitoring your behavior. It's likely that what you demonstrate, they will model. Remember, actions speak louder than words.

Treat people with dignity. When I supervised a team of 65, my boss always made me write up people needing discipline. I hated it. My boss encouraged me by letting me know how well I did it. It didn't make me feel better, but I began to wonder what I was doing differently that was so effective. Over the course of time, I realized one key was my empathy. Putting yourself in someone else's shoes is an important part of the discipline process. How would I want to be treated?

A man by the name of Gary Smalley once taught me a valuable lesson about people—the importance of valuing people or honoring them. As Gary was speaking before a group one day, he illustrated his point by passing a broken violin around for the audience to view. As the violin was passed around, people quickly glanced at it and handed it to the next person. Then, Gary explained that the violin, even in its broken condition was valuable, because if you looked inside the violin you could see a signature. The signature said, "Stradivarius."

The broken violin was worth several thousand dollars because of the signature inside. The audience then began to handle the violin with much more care and awe. Gary pointed out that when we look inside people we can see their real value and treat them with honor and respect, just as the audience was now treating the violin.

Here are some additional tips regarding discipline that I have found helpful:

- Praise in public and discipline in private.

- Remain calm. A calm explanation carries more weight than yelling and making a scene.

- Avoid using absolutes when disciplining. Absolutes create a sense of helplessness "You always…" "You never…" "You can't…"

- Leave a back door open. Changing behavior is more important than placing blame. When dealing with discipline, don't back people into a corner to hear them confess their guilt. Let them keep their dignity and keep the back door open for them to escape. For example: "I don't know if you did this deliberately or not, but the important thing is that it doesn't happen again. Do you agree?"

- Focus on what is important for the team or business. Discipline should not be personal if it can be avoided. It needs to be about how you and I can make the business better.

- Use the opportunity to positively encourage change: "I know you can do this, because you are such a dedicated worker."

- Don't hold a grudge. If they say they will change, do your best to believe them.

- Let them know the next action that will be taken as the result of a positive change and the result if there is no change at all.

- Follow up. If they improve, acknowledge how much you appreciate the improvement. If they do not improve, follow up with the next steps. "Follow up" is just another way to say "be consistent."

What About Virtual Teams?

You may be asking yourself, "Will this work if I'm supporting a remote or virtual team?" The answer is a resounding 'yes!' If you are leading a virtual team you are already aware of some of the unique challenges that having remote team members can present. Leading a virtual team will likely require you to work even harder as you lead and coach your team. Here are a few additional tips to consider when coaching a virtual team:

- Building trust with each of your team members is a critical key to the success of the team.
- Have regular scheduled team meetings honoring the different time zones of the team members.
- Communicate regularly and deliberately to the team and with each individual member.
  - Hold face-to-face sales meetings on a regular basis.
  - Leverage technology (conference calls, WebEx, Skype, and so on) for both team meetings and one-on-one communication to make meetings more personal.

Coaching virtually can be more challenging because you may have little chance to see remote team members "in action." You will not have visual clues to measure behavior and attitudes of remote team members, so trust is vital for both you and your team. Trust is best built through relationships. Relationships are best built by clear two-way communication.

Are you truly coaching to improve performance?

> ## Three-Step Checkup:
> - Have I provided proper training to the sales team and have I allowed enough time for them to become competent?
> - Have I established clear and consistent expectations for the sales team?
> - Do I consistently communicate my expectations to the team and do I properly handle team members that need improvement?

Summing It Up

I've focused on both the team, and the leader, but what does a good coaching session look like? Coaching should be a constant attitude, and not just something to do in a scheduled meeting. We want our teams to be the best salespeople they can be. When they are at their best, sales will increase as a byproduct of who they are.

Think about the best coach that you have ever known. Did you have an outstanding coach on a sports team you participated in as a child? Do you follow a college or professional team that has a great coach? Look at what they do right, and emulate what they do. Remember, watching a coach at game time is the smallest part of their coaching career. How do they handle the team when it's not game time? What does the team do to prepare to win? Now, think of your sales team and how you coach them. Their "game time" is when they are making the sales call, but you have to coach them on prospecting skills, product knowledge, and so on. There is so much coaching that happens beyond the sales call. Remember to:

- Praise and praise often. When praise is given with sincerity and honesty, it seldom creates an ego problem, so give it generously.
- Play to the strengths of the individual. Put the right person in the right position so they can succeed. Leverage their strengths and work as a team to compensate for areas of weakness.

- Provide honest feedback on a regular basis (both positive and constructive). If they don't get feedback from you, who are they getting it from?

- Share teachable moments during regular scheduled team meetings. Use team meetings as an opportunity to share a nugget of learning that may be of value to the team. Don't lecture or scold, just share. Allow others on the team to share and participate as well.

- Always be respectful of each individual team member, but do what is best for the team. You have a business to run and the team needs to understand the logic of the decision-making process. When possible, involve them in decision making.

There is no single magic bullet for coaching a team to increase their performance. It's hard work, but it is well worth the effort. You will find the work environment will be more enjoyable and the team more productive. In time, coaching will become natural and require less effort. Ask any winning team if they love their coach. You'll get any number of responses. Ask them if they enjoy winning, and everyone will respond with an affirmative "yes!" Winning coaches take the talent they have on the team and guide and develop them in such a way that they become champions.

Action Plan

1. Choose a coaching model (you will find options in an Internet search and your company may have one they use in training workshops).

    a. Review coaching models and use the one that will work best for you and your team. Most coaching models contain a few key elements in differing order. The order of these elements primarily impacts the order the steps in the coaching session and how these steps are delivered. I encourage you to incorporate these elements regardless of the model you use:

    - **Review and reflect on performance**: Both the manager and team member spend some time reflecting on and evaluating current and past performance.

- **Identify the performance gap:** What is the current state of the team member's performance and what should the future performance look like? The difference between the two is the performance gap. It's important to identify the gap so a resolution can be found.

- **Agree on action steps:** Agreement on the way to resolve the performance gap is the primary reason for having a coaching session. Performance needs to improve, and everyone needs to agree on the best method to make that improvement. It is also important to consider the consequences of not reaching the performance goal.

2. Consider attending an ASTD coaching certificate class to improve your sales coaching skills.

3. Read for personal development and share appropriate books you read with your team members.

References

Hersey, P. (1985). *The Situational Leader*. New York: Warner Books.

Arneson, J., W. Rothwell, and J. Naughton. (2013). "Training and Development Competencies Redefined to Create Competitive Advantage." *T+D*. www.astd.org/Publications/Magazines/TD/TD-Archive/2013/01/Training-and-Development-Competencies-Redefined.

Cofer, D.A. (2000). "Informal Workplace Learning." *Practice Application Brief*. www.calpro-online.org/eric/docs/pab00019.pdf.

ASTD Education. "Sales Coaching for Business Impact Certificate". www.astd.org/Education/Programs/Sales-Coaching-for-Business-Impact-Certificate.

About the Author

Leonard Cochran holds a bachelor's degree in adult education and has more than 15 years of experience managing teams ranging in size from 2 to 65. He began focusing on designing and developing sales training in 2009. He fell in love with the energy and excitement of working with the sales teams from the various Hilton Worldwide hotel brands and is now considered by some to be the resident expert on sales training. Today, he is employed as the learning programs manager for the commercial college as part of Hilton Worldwide University. Leonard is also an ASTD Certified Professional in Learning and Performance (CPLP) and actively serves in his local ASTD chapter.

3

Improving the Sales Call

Leo Tilley

It is easy for sales managers to be so busy meeting sales goals that they forget to slow down and take time to develop their people. Early in my career I made the same mistake until I was fortunate enough to have a good manager, who taught me how to focus on improving my sales reps, particularly in a sales call. The impact was amazing.

The purpose of this chapter is to provide actionable tips and ideas for a sales manager to use as they manage and coach the sales call process. I will cover the key steps of a good sales call, including:

- pre-call plan
- introduction

- uncovering or building needs
- making recommendations
- objections/concerns/negotiations
- closing
- debriefing the call.

At the end of each section, I will provide some manager tips and suggestions.

I feel the most important responsibility of a good sales manager is to help the sales reps prepare for their sales call and coach them after the call. The other responsibilities of a manager are important, but if a rep can't conduct a good sales call then all those other things don't mean anything. This is an area, however, where I've observed that sales managers do not spend enough time preparing. The worst managers jump in and take over the call thinking they are showing the rep what "good" looks like. Unfortunately, this usually results in upsetting the customer and the rep losing credibility.

Prior to starting the call you and the rep need to decide what your role will be. If you are going to help with the call then it will be difficult for you to also be the coach. To be an effective coach you need to sit back, observe, and take notes so you can provide good and specific feedback.

Pre-Call Plan

Let's start at the beginning with the pre-call plan. It is so important but is often overlooked by sales reps and sales managers. I was involved in a study where we worked with the sales executive board to measure activities where sales reps spent their time. The results showed that top reps spent more time doing pre-call plans than average reps. The outcome was that top reps were better prepared on what they wanted to accomplish and how they were going to do it during the sales call. They actually spent less time in the questioning phase of the sales call because they were able to ask well-focused questions that accomplished their call objectives.

They also had a very clear objective of what action they wanted the customer to take by the end of the call.

As a sales manager, this is a key area where you can help reps. Require them to do a pre-call plan for all of their calls. I remember doing a sales manager training program and telling the managers that. I got a lot of push back. They felt they should only require a pre-call plan on important calls—it would take too much time to do a pre-call plan for every call. Guess what happens when reps get that direction? Very few calls become important, so very few pre-call plans get done.

There was one manager in class who was quiet and I could tell he was paying attention. After the program, he came up to me and told me he was going to require his reps to start doing pre-call plans for all their calls. I checked in with him about a month later. He told me he got a lot of push back at the beginning but once they got into the habit, his reps saw the benefit and the results. Guess who the number one manager was that year?

There are lots of pre-call forms out there but I suggest you keep it simple. Here are a few key items to look for are in the pre-call plan.

Call Objective: What Action Do You Want the Customer to Take By the End of the Call?

This is important because it can be used to measure if the call was a successful. An example of a call objective might be: "I want the customer to introduce me to the key person involved in the purchasing process." The customer needs to take some action otherwise the sales process has not moved forward.

Add Value: How Are You Going to Add Value to the Customer?

The key to adding value is focusing on what problems or issues you plan to solve for the customer. The key question to ask the rep before the sales call is: "What problem do you want to solve for the customer?" If the rep doesn't know and the purpose of the call is to find out what problems the customer may have, that may be OK; but the rep must have some idea of what problems they want to uncover. If not, how do they know what questions they will ask to uncover problems? If they don't have a clue or a plan, they will typically ask a variety of questions and hope to find a problem. That usually doesn't work very well. Later we'll cover how to develop good questions that will focus in on the problems your products will solve.

Current Position: What Do You Know and What Do You Need to Know?

Prior to each sales call it is important to know what you want to find out. It's helpful if you have something you can easily remember. You can use the FARCD acronym as a memory aid.

"F" stands for what facts and frustrations. What do I want to uncover? Examples include current cost overruns, challenges, or changes in company direction, among others.

"A" stands for aspirations. What are their short- and long-term goals, personal, professional, departmental, and company? What do they want to accomplish?

"R" stands for resources. What is the budget time cycle? Who manages the budget?

"C" stands for competition. Who is your competition? Where do they stand in the account?

"D" stands for decision making. What is their decision-making process? Who is the key decision maker? What process did they go through the last time they made a decision like this? What kind of problems did they encounter?

"F" and "A" are factors that help you determine the customer's issues or problems and what they want to do about them. "R," "C," and "D" are factors that help you qualify the opportunity to see if you really want to focus on this account or not.

Questions: What Are You Going to Ask?

It's important to start working on the questions before, not during the call. Prior to the call I would always ask my reps what questions they were going to ask. Then I would respond as a customer might respond and ask the sales rep what he or she would say in response. Forcing them to articulate the questions and responses was very helpful. We often sound very erudite and smooth in our minds until we actually say the words. When you hear the words out loud they often don't come out as smoothly as you planned. Testing the language ahead of time is very helpful.

Pre-Call Plan Tips

- Make sure your reps get in the habit of doing a pre-call plan for every sales call.

- Ask what action the reps want the customer to take by the end of the sales call. If they don't know, don't go on the call until you develop one.

- Ask what problem they want to solve for the customer. If the customer doesn't perceive a problem, your solution will be irrelevant.

- Find out what they know and what they need to know. Use something like FARCD to check if they have everything covered.

- Review the questions they will ask. Prior to the call, role play questions and answers.

- Review potential objections or concerns and how you will deal with them. Role play answers.

- Prior to call, agree on what role you will play. You should be an observer not a key player.

Potential Objections/Questions: What Might You Run Into?

Maybe the customer is upset because of a backorder or missed shipment that you will need to take care of prior to moving ahead with the sales call. You need to be prepared for those issues so they don't derail your sales efforts.

Beginning the Call

When you walk into an office to see your customers, the first thing going through their minds, even if they know you well, is, "What does she want to talk to me about and do I really want to spend more than five minutes with this person?" Put yourself in their shoes, how do you feel when sales reps approach you? You know they want to sell you something because that's their job. It's important to help the rep set up the call in the beginning to prepare the customer, so you can get the best result in the end— and get the customer take action.

Beware of asking rapport questions too early. Or worse yet, spending too much time trying to develop a rapport. Research shows that customers know what you are doing and most don't appreciate it. I teach my reps to develop a rapport at the end of the call instead of at the beginning. I found this to be more effective because customers were more receptive after speaking for some time. Uncovering a problem and showing how you can help is the right way to get to know someone.

Here is a three step process for introducing yourself:

1. Tell them your name and who you work for. (You can skip this step, if the customer knows you well.)

2. Tell them your value proposition. By that I mean, what problems has your company been able to solve for customers in similar situations? Don't talk about products yet, focus on the problems. As a part of your pre-call prep you should have discovered certain issues that you know they must be dealing with. Remember, you're trying to give them a

reason to spend more than five minutes with you and answer your questions. Talk to them about something they care about.

3. Gain permission to ask questions. I also like to ask how much time we have in order to be respectful of their time.

Introduction Tips

- Help the reps understand the importance of properly introducing themselves. Get them to practice in front of you prior to the call.

- Review the potential problems that your value proposition will address prior to the call. Coach them to give the customer a good reason to spend more time with you.

- Observe and coach how the call is set up. A good set up makes customers more receptive to answering questions.

- Help the reps look for reasons to walk away. This will often be difficult for sales reps. This is an area where they will need your help.

- Things to watch for and give feedback during the debrief:

  - How well did they introduce themselves?

  - What was your perception of the customer reaction?

  - Did they provide a value proposition that the customer related to?

  - Did they get permission to ask questions?

Uncovering and Building Needs

This is all about asking good questions to create a need in the customer's mind. This is the most important part of the sales call. The goal is to ask good questions that make connections for the customers so they tell you their needs and problems. People remember, and believe much more of what they say, than what a rep says. They also value information they ask for more than information that is freely given. So that means in order to increase the success rate of a call, you need to help the customer come to conclusions that help them uncover a problem or need. You also need to create a sense of urgency to solve those problems. If you do it right, you build up the problems and needs to the point where the customer is asking you for a solution. It's not easy to wait that long, but when done right, it's extremely successful.

I had the opportunity to experience one of the best sales calls I have ever seen while I was the director of training for the clinical division at Kodak. I had two gentlemen meet with me to sell me a training program. They spent an hour and a half just asking me questions about my training programs. Not once did they talk about their product. They got me to the point where I realized my training programs needed a lot of help. I was practically begging them to tell me their solution. They refused to give me their solution until they came back a week later with their proposal. Their solution aligned perfectly with my training needs. Guess what? Price wasn't an issue. They had built up my problems to the point that I would have paid anything to get them fixed. They did an excellent job in creating a sense of urgency to solve problems that I didn't realize I had.

Too often I've observed sales reps doing a good job of uncovering or developing a need, but their product or solution won't solve it. Then they are up a creek without a paddle. There is a great exercise a friend showed me several years ago to develop good questions that will focus on problems you can solve. On a sheet of paper or flip chart draw a line down the middle. At the top of the left-hand side write "Features." Then down the left-hand side write the most important features of your product or service. Don't go crazy, five or six will do. Then at the top of the right-hand side write "Problems." In the right-hand sections answer the question, "What problems would someone have if they did not have that feature?" Now that you have the problems, you're ready to develop the questions. Asking good questions is essential and this is where the sales manager can show value as a coach.

When coaching a sales call there are many things to watch out for. Here is a list of behaviors and actions that reps should avoid:

- **Asking too many questions about information the reps should already know.** In other words, if the reps had done a little more pre-work and research into the customer, they wouldn't be asking these questions. It isn't the customer's job to educate the reps. To grab—and hold on to—the customer's attention, you need to get them talking about their problems or issues. The sooner you can get to questions that pertain to things they are paid to do, the better. A good manager early in my sales career gave me some excellent advice. He said, "If you want to know how to sell to someone, ask questions to find out why they were hired, or what were they were hired to do, how they are measured, and what could get them fired." If you know these things you'll know how to create a sense of urgency.

- **Asking too many close-ended questions that can be answered by "yes" or "no."** So many reps fall into this trap because these are easy questions to ask; however, they require more follow-up questions or could disrupt your sales call entirely if you receive an answer you don't want to hear. In most cases it is very easy to take a close-ended question and make it open ended, simply by adding only one or two words such as why, how, or who. Here's an example:

  - Close-ended question: "Do you have a problem with X, Y, and Z?" That can be changed to: "How do you deal with the problems with X, Y, and Z?" Now if they reply they don't have that problem, you can say, "That's great. Can you tell me why not? What are you doing to prevent having that problem?" Either way you get the customer saying much more than a simple "yes" or "no."

- **Asking a string of questions without giving the customer a chance to answer.** I see this more often from very experienced reps that have a strong knowledge of their field. This also happens when reps are nervous or anxious because they have so much to say that they can't stop from saying it all at once. By the time they are finished, the customer is so confused they don't know which question to answer.

- **Not asking enough questions around the implications once they uncover a problem.** Did the rep ask more questions to build up the problem or did he jump in with their solution immediately after uncovering a problem? Are the customers answering with a lot of objections?

This usually happens because the rep hasn't created a sense of urgency and is offering solutions too soon.

- **Missing problems that customers mention because they are too focused on showing their product.** I often see reps so intent on talking about their product that a customer will mention a problem that we have a solution for—and the rep will totally ignore it so that he can talk about what he wanted to talk about. That's what I call "product-focused" instead of "customer-focused." It's a shame but it happens a lot. The managers are part of the problem. Often the manager is pushing the rep to sell more of a particular product to hit a quota or budget, so the rep focuses only on selling that product, to the detriment of everything else.

- **Asking solution questions or presenting your solution too early.** The usual response to these questions is some reason why the customers don't want to or can't commit at that time. That's commonly known as an objection. This happens because the rep has not developed the need to the point where the customer wants to do something about it. That's where asking more questions about the consequences of the problem are the key to getting the customer's need level to the point of taking action. Top sales reps hold off presenting the solution until they recognize the customer will be most receptive.

- **Asking leading questions.** For instance: "So doctor, if I could show you a pill that will totally eliminate your surgical site infections, cure cancer, and eliminate your marital problems, would you buy it?" Questions like that make me sick. I see those most often from pharmaceutical reps. They are trained to ask questions that the customer would have to be an idiot to say "no" to. They are manipulative and leading questions and as a customer I would be offended.

Making Recommendations

When it's time to make your recommendation, hopefully the rep hasn't jumped the gun and started too soon. This is when, as a manager, you can observe how he presents the solution. First he should summarize all the needs he uncovered and get confirmation that those are all the needs the customer wants to address. Then the rep should discuss just the benefits and features that address those needs. A common problem I see is when the rep can't wait to tell the customer about all the great features he has to offer. The problem this can create is if he talks about a feature that doesn't address a need, then it probably doesn't have any value to the customers and they won't want to pay for it. Why should they? That's when you get price objections.

Uncovering and Building Needs Tips

Take notes! I can't emphasize this enough. I often see managers sit through an entire sales call and not take one note. This habit prevents the manager from giving useful feedback, and sets a poor example (if the manager doesn't think it's important to take notes, why should reps). There is no way you can give specific feedback unless you take good notes. The manager is forced to give generic feedback, such as "You did a good job with your opening and your questions." That's not helpful! You have to tell them exactly what they did that was good. What question did they ask that worked so well? It's even more important when you discuss the things they didn't do well. Without specifics your feedback is useless.

During the call, you should write down the needs or problems uncovered. It will be important to have this to reference when you ask the rep what they uncovered. See if they are able to articulate the same needs or problems that you observed.

Observe and measure who talks more in the sales call. Studies have shown—and my experience has confirmed—that in successful sales calls, the customer does most of the talking. If the rep is doing most of the talking then you need to help them ask better questions. A lot of the time reps agonize over asking long, involved questions when a simple question like, "Why?" or "How often?" works much better to get the customer to talk more. The simpler the better. This is one area the manager can really observe and help.

Objections/Resolving Concerns/Negotiations

This is one area where reps can use a lot of help. Many sales training programs teach reps to handle objections by using a three- or four-step process that they need to memorize.

These processes look great on paper, but whoever put them together never had to actually use them. In the middle of a sales call reps don't have the time to mentally think through the steps to find a response. That just isn't realistic. When a sales call gets tense they have to respond quickly and accurately. That usually comes with practice and good coaching.

Recommendation/Proposal Tips

Here are some things to watch out for when the rep makes their recommendation:

- Did the rep summarize and confirm all the customer needs before presenting solutions?
- Did the rep accurately articulate all the customer needs?
- Did the rep start with the customer needs or did she start with how great your company is and how your products will solve all their needs?
- Did the rep present all the features that addressed the specific customer needs?
- If she got a lot of objections, ask "What were they and why?"

Often when a rep gets an objection, I see him or her trying to show the customers how their perception is wrong and then try to justify their proposal. It seems the harder you push to show your value, the harder the customer pushes to deny it. When you try to justify your stance and the customer disagrees, the customer often launches a vigorous contradiction. In response, you defend your position. The sales call spirals and usually ends in a stalemate.

Here is something I learned from a top-notch negotiating class that has always worked very well. When presented with a viewpoint opposite to yours, never argue right away. Arguing at this point simply invites retaliation. The harder you disagree, the deeper your opponent digs in. Then it becomes a battle of egos—no one wants to be proven wrong!

Here's a simple three step plan:

1. Acknowledge the other party.

2. Show partial agreement with their stance.

3. Smoothly insert your views.

Objections/Resolving Concerns/Negotiations Tips

- Practice overcoming objections prior to the sales call. Here is another area where you can add value. You should come up with as many objections as you can think of after reviewing the pre-call plan. A manager has a lot of experience seeing and handling objections based on their own experience and observing other calls. Prior to the call, throw out typical objections and ask the rep how he will respond. Make sure the rep gives you a verbal response of exactly how he would say it to the customer. What comes out of your mouth is never as smooth as what is in your head. So if he says, "I would tell them about A and B." You should say "No, respond to me exactly as you would to the customer." If the response isn't good or you know of a better response, make him do it until it rolls off his tongue smoothly. Practice makes perfect.

- Observe to see if the rep uses the "feel, felt, found technique" or if he tries to justify his position with more features and facts. Show him the impact on the customer when he tries to push his solution instead of showing understanding about how the customer feels first.

Master negotiators call this the "feel, felt, found technique." Commit this to memory and you can easily and naturally recover from any objection or argument. This avoids presenting a "let me show you what a stupid idiot you are" response, which just invites retaliation or push back.

Here is what it looks like:

Buyer: "I don't think I'll take your product. Your price is too high."

You: "I can understand exactly how you feel because others have felt exactly the same way. But you know what they've found? We offer the widest array of free aftermarket support and unparalleled warranties. They keep coming back."

Debriefing the Call

Now is the time for the coaching part of the job to begin. It is very important to do it right. One of the best training programs I took in my career was a sales coaching training program. The key takeaway and most useful process I learned was the correct way to debrief a call. I learned to ask a series of questions that enabled me to effectively review and coach the sales call.

A key point is to ask the right questions in the right order to get the sales rep to do most of the talking. Remember earlier when I said people believe more what they say than what they are told? That goes for sales reps too. In the debrief you want the rep to do most of the talking.

Great coaches help people learn by discovery. The key to any coaching session, therefore, is to ask the right questions to get the sales rep to realize the correct course of action and verbalize it themselves. I once heard a coach say, "If I have to tell them what to do, I've failed as a coach." I think that's a bit drastic, but the core is correct. Of course, you'll always have the rep or two that just don't get it and you just have to tell them what to do.

Five Effective Debriefing Questions

1. Did you accomplish your sales call objective?

2. What do you think you did well in the call?

3. What would you do differently, if you could do it over again?

4. What action is the customer taking as a result of this call?

5. What are your next steps to move this sale forward?

You need to be careful when starting the debrief. It is very important to focus on the positive first. Typically the reps will want to talk about things they should have done or how they messed up this or that. It's important of focus on what they did right first! You can agree and reinforce what they did well and hopefully add a few additional items that they did right and forgot to mention. Remember give them specifics! That shows you were observing and making good use of your notes.

Then ask what they would do differently if they could do it over again. Let them talk, and typically, they will be much harder on themselves than you would. Your next question should be, "Now what do you think you should do to improve?" If they don't get it, then you have to make suggestions. Remember the more talking they do, the more they will get out of it and the longer they will remember it.

As far as frequency and timing of the debrief, I recommend you do it for every call, and start once you leave the building and on the way to the next call. Don't wait until the end of the day, that won't work well at all. If you get in the habit of asking those five questions after every call, the sales reps will know automatically to start thinking that way. I would encourage my reps to ask themselves those same questions after every call they make. It's a great way to debrief what just happened, how you performed, and prepare for future calls.

> # Debriefing Tips
>
> - Get in the habit of asking the five questions or any version that you like after every call.
> - Debrief as soon as possible after the call and before the next call. This will actually help you prepare for the next call.
> - Don't debrief in the car while the rep is driving. He or she needs to focus on driving safely.

The job of a sales manager is very complex and involves many different skills and areas of expertise. The most important part of the job, however, is developing people, particularly on how to conduct a successful sales call. If they can't conduct a good sales call, all the rest of their skills aren't going to mean much. Hopefully, I have been able to give you some good tips and ideas to help you develop your sales reps to improve their sales calls and overall sales success.

Good luck and good selling!

Summing It Up

When I was first trained in sales eons ago, it was the old ABC method: Always Be Closing. Throughout the call I was taught to ask for small closes like, "You do you agree that this could help with … don't you?" You were supposed to ask a lot of what I call leading questions so at the end, when you asked for the order, it would be difficult for them to say "no" because they have been saying "yes" so many times before. Then we were taught all the different techniques to get them to sign the order like the Ben Franklin Close, the Assumptive Close, the Puppy Dog Close, and so on. They were all very manipulative and most customers caught on and didn't appreciate it. Good sales techniques continue to evolve just as our customers' decision-making processes continue to evolve. In the current sales environment of more complex sales and more complex decision processes, it takes several calls before you can get an order. Therefore, it becomes very important that each sales call has as much impact as possible to drive the process forward. The best way to make that happen is to make sure the customer takes some type of action at the end of each call. If the customer doesn't take an action, the sales process has not progressed.

Moving the process forward can be as simple as picking up the phone and introducing the rep to another person in the decision-making process, or agreeing to and actually giving you some information, or agreeing to and actually setting up another meeting with key individuals. As the rep moves through the process, those actions get more detailed, difficult, and decisive—such as agreeing to eliminate the competition from the decision-making process. As a sales manager, you may need to help your rep decide on the most advanced customer action you want to achieve in each sales call. The beauty of it is that you have something concrete you can measure at the end of the call. Asking about the action at the end of the call should be your first question when you debrief.

Closing Tips

- Prior to the call, get agreement on what action you want to take at the end of the sales call. Have the rep practice how she will ask for the close. The more reps practice prior to the call, the smoother they will be in the call.

- Observe who talks first after the close. Silence is painful for most sales reps. When a customer doesn't say anything the rep often gets uncomfortable and starts talking. Bad move. Sometimes, particularly when you are closing, the customer needs a little time to think. Make sure the rep gives them that time. I was taught early in my sales career to close and keep my mouth closed until the customer spoke. It's tough, but it works. Practice when a rep asks you a question; hesitate answering to see how long it takes for her to say something. This is a good coaching opportunity.

Action Plan

Helping Improve Sales Calls:

1. Evaluate strengths and opportunities for improvement for each sales rep.

2. Share your evaluation with the sales rep and get their buy-in. Ask them where they think they need to improve. You may be surprised.

3. Set up a time to travel with each rep and decide what you will coach during the trip.

4. Build a simple spreadsheet that you leave with the sales rep to track progress to include:

    - objective

    - action

    - target date

    - status.

About the Author

Leo Tilley is the director of global performance and learning at Kimberly-Clark Health Care. He has more than 30 years of experience in the medical device environment with world-class companies including: Kodak, Johnson & Johnson, Boston Scientific, and Kimberly Clark. His experience includes sales, sales management, training, training management, marketing, and distributor channel management along with an international assignment in Japan. Leo is certified in instruction design and selling processes including SPIN and Customer Oriented Selling. He has developed and facilitated advanced selling and sales management training programs around the globe.

4

Managing the Sales Team Pipeline

Steve Gielda

What do we need to do to make sales forecasting more accurate? This is one of the most common and urgent questions asked by senior sales leaders. In theory, the answer is rather simple; but in practice, getting better forecasts has proven extremely challenging.

Aligning the Processes

So what's the underlying problem? The dots aren't connected. The most common reason sales managers can't get sales reps to forecast more accurately is because the company sales process isn't represented in the pipeline stages. The company's sales pipeline process does not align with the company's sales process. Too often companies implement a sales pipeline process without any regard for the fundamental and strategic activities that take place throughout the sales process. In this chapter, I will provide some simple ideas to help you better align your sales process to your pipeline process and better leverage your pipeline process as a sales coaching tool.

The science of human performance technology teaches us that performance problems in the workplace generally boil down to three overarching factors: attitude, skills, and knowledge. Attitude has to do with whether the workers are motivated to do the task; it's the why. Skills, of course, are about ability; they are the how. And knowledge is about understanding; we might call that the what. When workers are not satisfactorily performing the tasks that are required, it boils down to gaps in the why, how, and what, and the interplay between them. However, when it comes to complex tasks demanded of an entire enterprise (for example, pipeline management for a large-scale salesforce), a fourth element becomes essential for good forecasting: a well-thought-out, validated, and repeatable process. And it's been my experience that many sellers—and many organizations—simply lack a reliable and consistent way to predict which deals will close and when. Producing an accurate forecast becomes a sort of meteorological art, but without the reliability. It's no wonder sellers resist doing them. And it's no wonder managers are frustrated. Nobody's getting what they really want or need from the effort. To borrow a phrase used in reengineering and total quality management (TQM), blame the process, not the people.

Many of you are probably thinking that the only purpose of the pipeline process is so senior sales leaders can keep track of who's working and who's not. More than one salesperson has expressed sentiments like this IT sales rep: "Forecasting has no value to me. My manager just wants it so he has something to hold over my head until the end of the month." This may be more true than managers care to admit because bad information from bad pipeline management processes yield forecasts that have little value for anyone, except as an enforcement tool. However, there is tremendous value in managing your customer opportunities in an active and strategic pipeline management process. Emerging customer relationship management (CRM) software, such as SalesForce, SAP, Siebel, and others, have made great strides in simplifying the reporting process. This ought to have led to better forecasts and improved pipeline management. Yet the problems persist and sales reps and managers still have challenges getting the results everyone wants.

Finding the Problem

Good technology layered over processes that don't work yields unsatisfactory results.

Too often companies implement a sales pipeline process into their organization to match their shiny new CRMs, without any regard to the core strategic sales activities that sales reps should be completing throughout the entire process.

Most pipeline or funnel management systems use terms such as Stage 1, Stage 2, Stage 3, and Stage 4, or the even more vague Early Cycle, Mid-Cycle, and Late Cycle. We have seen five-stage models. We have seen seven-stage models. We have even seen a 12-stage model. It doesn't matter how many stages the process has (five seems to be a pretty common "magic number"), but our evidence tends to be anecdotal and experiential, rather than statistically significant. The problems arise not from the number of stages there are, but rather murkiness around each stage's definition. If, for one constituency Stage 1 means "targeting and qualifying," but for another it means "uncovering needs," the pipeline's results will be ambiguous at best. A process whose boundaries and stage definitions can shift from constituency to constituency, or case by case, is a process that does not work. But when a clearly defined pipeline process aligns perfectly with sales activities, the results can be stunning.

When the Pipeline Hums

I saw this success story play out while working with a global commercial bank solution provider. Heather was the North American VP of sales, and she was striving valiantly to improve her team's forecasting. After building a more rigorous pipeline process, not only did she get a more accurate sales forecast, but also the added benefit of a more strategically minded sales team.

Heather's North American sales team consisted of nearly 250 sales reps and their 30 sales managers. Like many organizations, forecasting was about as accurate as guessing when double zero would come up on the roulette table. Sales reps didn't have an effective or consistent way to predict when their opportunities would close. Each region had its own way of doing things. This caused many problems for Heather, to say nothing of her company. Her biggest concern was providing a more accurate sales forecast to her senior management team each quarter. If projections were off by more than 5 percent in either direction, Heather had to explain and justify it, a verbal shuffle that brought about a rapid heartbeat and nervous sweats. She asked us to help her develop a pipeline process that would consistently provide accurate forecasts to the senior management team.

We began with data collection. We interviewed Heather's top-performing sales directors, regional managers, and sales reps across the sales organization to learn three things. First, how they were communicating with each other about where the customer was in their decision process. Second, how they defined the stages or steps in the process. What sort of ground rules were they using to move customers out of one stage and into another? Third, we wanted to know what managers were doing to be a value-adding resource throughout the process.

At the time, the company did not have a central pipeline process across the organization. Some regions did it one way, some did it another. But among the top performers, there emerged a consistent theme. These top performers utilized a consistent and rigorous process for their region, whether it involved five pipeline stages or 10, and they communicated frequently about progress—or lack thereof—through the pipeline's stages.

The unfortunate reality, though, was that the top performers were not any more successful at forecasting than average or below-average performers were. For Heather, this was not acceptable. So working in collaboration with a cross-functional team, we designed and implemented a rigorous, workable five-stage sales pipeline. The five stages were:

Table 4.1

Stage 1	Stage 2	Stage 3	Stage 4	Stage 5
Opportunity Qualification	Needs Development	Solution Identification	Implementation Resolution	Contract Confirmation

The five stages were not a miraculous revelation. They weren't even particularly innovative. They were just five stages, with no magic attached to the number five.

There was power, of course, in the model's simplicity, especially considering scalability, applicability, and repeatability. If your pipeline model is so complex you need to hire engineers to make sense of it, it will become useless. Our five stages had the advantage of being so simple that anyone can understand and use them. Another advantage of our model was clarifying boundaries between the stages themselves. What impressed Heather—and what made this approach different from some of the company's approaches in the past—was the clear and unambiguous way in which the five stages were delineated, and the key milestones and metrics built into each stage.

Agreeing upon the number of stages in your sales pipeline—and naming them in a way that is both memorable and denotative—is indeed a critical first step, but it is only the first step. More important than fixing on the right number of stages is clearly defining each of them. What constitutes the first stage? And how is it distinct from the second? What criteria have to be met to move an opportunity from Stage 3 to Stage 4? What key milestones have to be passed, what activities have to take place? These criteria—the activities and milestones— ought to reflect the day-to-day selling activities of your sales rep. For example, is making contact at the C-level a necessary activity? If so, it ought to be a milestone in one of the stages (for example, "Met with C-level buyers and identified company's goals"). Is mapping all the key players important to your team? If so, it too ought to be a milestone ("Identified my adversaries and developed a plan to win their support").

So, coupled closely with naming and defining each stage is ensuring that the pipeline process integrates with the day-to-day activities in the sales process. That is, selling activities should fit with the pipeline. Connecting the dots for Heather's company gave them a process that was workable for the entire sales team, leading to positive changes in Heather's forecasting accuracy.

Establishing the crucial milestones for each stage makes it easier for salespeople and managers to communicate with clarity where they are in the pipeline process. When Harry tells his manager Sally that ACME, Inc., is a Stage 3 opportunity, Harry is telling Sally that each of the milestones in Stages 1 and 2 have been met. With a bit of discussion, Sally will know how close ACME, Inc., is to graduating to Stage 4. This is where the pipeline process becomes a great coaching tool. Sally, being a smart sales manager, will ask Harry a series of smart, strategic coaching questions that can truly assess whether or not ACME, Inc., actually belongs in Stage 3. If one of the milestones in Stage 2 was to "Identify the customer's decision criteria and establish a strategy to better position our company value," Sally may ask Harry, "What was your customer decision criteria and which of our unique capabilities align best with the customer?" If Harry isn't able to provide his manager with a smart and accurate response there is a good chance Harry skipped that milestone. Another milestone might be "Develop strategy to neutralize your adversaries." Here Sally may ask her rep, "Who have you identified as your adversaries that have a high level of influence and what was your strategy to neutralize their perception of our company?"

Managing the sales pipeline effectively requires sales managers to know how to challenge their reps. To merely ask them if they completed all of the milestones in a previous stage is actually insulting. The job of the manager is to help the sales rep identify why that milestone is important and how to leverage that information to secure the opportunity.

On the following page is a list of a few strategic coaching questions we have picked up from our clients over the years; these questions are designed to challenge the sales rep, to get them to think about the opportunity at a deeper level.

Keeping the process simple is important. It seems that in the corporate world, simplicity is a bad sign. If it's simple, it must not be complete. But it's important to remember that simplicity is crucial with processes that need to be scaled across large enterprises.

An effective pipeline process needs to combine simplicity with effectiveness; it must not only be easy to learn and apply across a population of users, it must be robust enough to stand up to day-to-day sales rigors. As we've discussed, the challenge is in thoroughly defining each stage, delineating them from one another, and clearly distinguishing their boundaries. The key task in this endeavor is identifying the proper milestones within each stage. The milestones comprise the tasks that must be completed before moving on. What comes before what? For example, it has been well established that it's important to understand early in the sales process who the key players are in the account, and what their roles are in the decision. A subsequent step might involve defining the customer's selection criteria.

10 Smart, Strategic Coaching Questions

1. What concerns you most about the customer's decision criteria, and what is your strategy to alleviate these concerns?

2. What assumptions might you have made regarding these decision criteria? How can you validate your assumptions?

3. What is your strategy to win support for those who are adversary? What are the barriers that could preclude that from happening?

4. What are some things that the adversaries value? How can we influence those things?

5. If there are multiple decision makers, do they all agree on the same selection criteria? Who's selection criteria matters most and why?

6. In what selection criteria is the competition stronger? What is your strategy to strengthen our position in these areas?

7. Which market trends are having the greatest impact on this customer? How will it affect our sales efforts?

8. What responsibility do these stakeholders have to help their company take advantage of, or combat trends, in the market?

9. What actions might the competition take that could hurt our efforts inside this account?

10. What metrics will your customer use to measure the value of your solution?

A Fully-Functional Pipeline

Let's go back to Heather's situation. We ended up developing a five-stage pipe-line process that included critical milestones and tasks for each phase of the process. On the following page is Heather's pipeline process as we designed it.

Table 4.2

Stage 1 Opportunity Qualification	Stage 2 Needs Development	Stage 3 Solution Identification	Stage 4 Implementation Resolution	Stage 5 Contract Confirmation
Identified advocates and adversaries	Needs and downside risks identified	Financial buyer contacted	Implementation risks identified and addressed	Hard copy PO received
All players involved in decision process identified	Strategy to neutralize adversaries implemented	Decision criteria validated	Reconfirmed with advocates that all iceberg issues are handled	Paperwork sent to order entry
Decision factors identified	Confirmed where buyer is in decision process	Buyers understand the link between final solution and their needs	Confirmed that stakeholders have taken ownership for solution	Confirmed the purchase and delivery process
Nature and severity of buyer concern identified	Decision criteria identified	Competitive analysis completed; strategy for influencing decision criteria defined	Final presentation made to decision team	Implementation and client training plan confirmed
	Compelling reason to act identified	"Go-no-Go" decision discussed with customer		
	Availability of estimated budget confirmed			

Implementing this pipeline process had five distinct advantages for Heather and her company:

- **Sales reps are clear about their call objective before the sales call begins.** Too often average performers walk in and out of their customers' offices without doing anything strategic or intentional to drive the customer closer to a decision. With clear milestones in each stage of the pipeline process, Heather's team was able to check which milestones had not been passed for that stage, and then develop a smart call plan to achieve those objectives. For example, if a sales rep has an opportunity in Stage 3 and one of the milestones is to validate the customer's decision criteria, then the call objective is clear.

- **It shortens the sales cycle.** Top sales reps are proactively driving their customers' buying processes, versus playing a passive or reactive role. The pipeline process implements smart and clear milestones at each stage. This fosters momentum-building activities because sales reps are motivated to get the customers to take action.

- **The sales reps and their manager have absolute clarity about where the opportunity is in the pipeline.** An opportunity cannot move into Stage 3 until it has met all the criteria for Stage 2. A rep cannot promote an opportunity to an advanced stage before its time, so nobody gets false optimism about a deal's likeliness to close.

- **Sales managers can quickly identify where a sales rep may need help.** Too often sales managers spend hours conducting "account reviews" with their teams without having any clear objectives for the conversation. Establishing criteria for each stage of the pipeline process allows the manager to quickly identify which accounts seem to be stuck in the pipeline. They can collaborate with their reps on developing action plans to move the opportunity forward. Without milestones in each stage of the pipeline, managers may conduct account reviews with good intentions, but they can't establish which direction the seller should move to secure the business opportunity.

- **Establishing clear milestones in each stage of the pipeline process creates a set of forecast metrics that the sales rep can rely on.** The manager knows if he can get his entire team to use the pipeline process that was established and coaches his team to achieve the milestones in each stage of the pipeline process, everyone will win.

The pipeline model we designed for Heather quickly improved the company's forecasting accuracy, to say nothing of the sales team's increased interest in using the process. Heather and her sales managers became more aware of the warning signs of an opportunity stalling or slowing. Conversely, they were able to respond more efficaciously when an opportunity's forward momentum increased because they saw it coming. Over time, Heather and her management team established reliable metrics that gave them insight into their business. For instance, they learned that opportunities that entered Stage 3 had a 78 percent chance of closing. When the opportunity moved into Stage 4, the percentage jumped to 86 percent. Heather was able to provide her senior management team the accurate forecast they were demanding. More importantly, her sales reps and sales managers had a consistent pipeline process.

Summing It Up

Sales forecasting is inevitably problematic. Some salespeople are too optimistic. Some are too pessimistic. And beyond optimism and pessimism is plain, old forecasting ineptitude. The end result is inaccurate forecasts. This chapter provided some tools and techniques for improving your pipeline management process by helping you see the importance of building critical milestones into each stage. These milestones help create a common understanding of the pipeline process.

Action Plan

Putting a smart pipeline process in place isn't difficult, but it does take some careful consideration. We suggest you follow this easy three-step process to get started:

1. Categorize the stages of your pipeline. We've found through experience that these five tend to work across nearly every sales sector. They are:

Table 4.3

Stage 1	Stage 2	Stage 3	Stage 4	Stage 5
Opportunity Qualification	Needs Development	Solution Identification	Implementation Resolution	Contract Confirmation

You may incorporate more or less than five stages in your pipeline model. However, more important than determining how many stages there should be is defining what criteria you use to promote a prospect from one stage to the next. This leads us to step two.

2. Agree on the criteria that defines each stage. We advise that these criteria be clearly defined and aligned with the necessary activities that create value for your solutions. For example, if gaining access to the C-suite and conducting an economic value conversation are important, be sure to include these as part of your criteria.

    Having the right criteria that both clearly define the specific stage of the pipeline and drive your sales process is important, but ensuring your sales team understands the value of the process is also important. Salespeople often believe that pipeline management tools are only important for sales leaders. Your sales team needs to understand the value to them. Without clear understanding, you will struggle with driving accountability among your sales team, which leads us to Step 3.

3. Once you have the stages categorized and clearly defined with smart criteria, ask your sales reps to select their top 10 accounts and place each of them into the stage that best aligns where they are in the sales process. Ask them to be honest with themselves and be careful not to put an opportunity late in the pipeline process if they haven't met the criteria in the early stages. This exercise will help your reps better identify steps in the sales process they might have skipped. Only ask your team to add their top 10 accounts because they may get a little overwhelmed after they recognize they have missed many of the crucial criteria in each stage.

    Accountability is key. Top sales managers hold their teams accountable for meeting the criteria in each stage before allowing them to advance the opportunity. If you have established the criteria that drives your sales process and you hold your team accountable for meeting those criteria, you will not only improve your forecasting, you will also improve your closing ratio!

About the Author

Steve Gielda is the principal partner at Ignite Selling, Inc., a global sales training and consulting company and author of *Premeditated Selling: Tools for Developing the Right Strategy for Every Opportunity*. Steve has spent more than 20 years helping Fortune 1000 companies in the healthcare, manufacturing, distribution, and IT industries to improve their sales performance. His emphasis on building and maintaining strong relationships and his focus on driving business results is what sets him apart with his clients. Steve began his career in sales with Lanier Worldwide, a document management solutions company, eventually becoming a regional manager. He was also vice president of sales and channel management at CTN, an office equipment manufacturing and distribution company. After CTN, Steve worked as a senior sales consultant for Huthwaite, helping to create unique sales training solutions for his clients. Most recently, he was a franchise owner with the Advantage Performance Group consulting and learning firm, and an active partner in building the business of Sales Momentum, a customized sales training organization.

5
Selling Across Cultures

Anup Soans and Joshua Soans

In 1991, India opened up its markets to the world economy, bringing a billion people into the global market. They were made up of over 2,000 ethnicities, 1,576 "mother tongues," eight major religions, and thousands of local dietary and religious practices. Multinationals entering the Indian market would have to successfully navigate this cultural jungle to survive and thrive.

The fact that McDonald's, the world's largest seller of beef products, has a thriving business in India, the land of the sacred cow, is proof that cultural differences are only a barrier when a company fails in its due diligence. McDonald's has a strict "no-beef, no-pork" policy in India because the cow is widely worshipped by Hindus and consumption of pork is forbidden in Islam. Instead, the fast-food chain has a variety of vegetarian and chicken dishes in local flavors and is considered to be just as Indian by urbanites as curry and naan. Because of its cultural astuteness the world over, McDonald's has become the poster child for "glocalization"—the art of being global in character but local in spirit.

In her book *111 Ideas to Engage Global Audiences*, Renie McClay says, "there is not a 'there' when learning about other cultures. You don't learn everything about a culture." What businesses do need to factor in when selling across cultures are the "known knowns" and "known unknowns" of cultural behaviors.

A key role for sales managers is to help sellers "translate" their sales process into the language and practices of their customers to be effective. A simple Internet search on "selling to different cultures" will bring up several pages of useful information. Some important questions to ask when selling to different cultures are:

- How much time on average does it take to build trust and relationships with customers?
- How important are references and which references will carry more weight?
- How direct can you be with your questioning and probing?
- How strongly can you push the advantages and benefits of your product or service?
- How strongly can you push for a commitment from the customer?

Self-Awareness for the Seller

Knowledge of one's own cultural preferences and tendencies is the starting point for understanding and appreciating those of others. There are many ways to do this. A formal understanding of culture is always useful (and quite interesting!) if you have the time.

Since the pioneering work of Geert Hofstede in the 1970s, much work has been done on mapping out the cultural tendencies of countries and social groups using Hofstede's parameters of power distance, individualism, uncertainty avoidance, masculinity, and long-term orientation.

- Power distance is the degree to which social hierarchy is accepted and expected to be adhered to.

- Individualism is the degree to which individual behavior and responsibility is emphasized versus collective or group behavior and responsibility.

- Uncertainty avoidance measures a society's preference for regularity and systems versus ambiguity.

- Masculinity is the degree to which a society is imbued with "masculine" values like competition and heroism versus "feminine" values like cooperation and modesty.

- Long-term orientation can be interpreted as a society's preference for absolute truths and tradition (doing the right thing in the short run) at the cost of contextual aptness versus a preference for practicable and amicable solutions with a focus on long-term stability and relationships.

A recent addition to these five parameters is indulgence versus restraint. The former stands for a society that encourages the basic human drives for pleasure and fun and the latter for societies that privilege stoicism and self-control. Even a bare minimum understanding of where one's own culture scores on these parameters can be an eye-opener. The Hofstede Centre website is a good place to start for those who want to better understand the cultural dimensions listed above and see how different countries compare.

Accounting for the Hofstede's dimensions while selling across cultures might seem like a daunting task, but like any skill, mastery is a function of awareness and practice. This is an area sales managers need to learn and excel and then they can help their sales teams to do the same.

For example, Americans doing business in Japan (as in many countries), need to adjust their normal selling practices. Expecting to close a deal with one or maybe two sales calls is not a reasonable expectation. You will build trust by repeatedly getting to know them, likely including social events for the purpose of getting to know each other. They are not just buying your product; they are buying the company and the individuals they will be working with.

In Latin America you gain favor with a referral from someone the prospect respects, so your network becomes vitally important there.

Alfredo Castro was teaching a sales workshop in Brazil to 12 directors from the same company, half from Brazil and half from Europe and Asia. The Brazilians had powerful narratives for engaging the other person in sales dialogue. They established a strong emotional connection and provided great reasons for doing business together. It was a very different approach from the Europeans and Asians, but they had to admit it had a positive impact on doing business and getting a "yes" from their customers.

Tips for Sellers

- Use Hofstede's Dimensions to clearly map out your cultural preferences and those of your customers and see how they compare.

- Which are the areas where your cultural preferences and the preferences of your customer are likely to be at odds?

- Culture aside, do your personality traits favor any of the above mentioned cultural preferences? For example, are you someone who prefers order and regularity in your business dealings or are you comfortable with ambiguity and open-endedness? Are these traits in sync with the cultural tendencies of the customer (a strength to be played up) or are they at odds (a weakness to be mindful about)?

- Is there someone from the local culture whom you can trust? Is that person familiar with your culture or better still, you? You might want to play out a critical scenario with him or her. There are also many professional service providers who can perform this role.

These questions are great for discussing in sales meetings, with new salespeople, and with veterans who are selling to a new geography or culture.

Be Clear and Forthright About Your Core Values

It is easy to fall prey to cultural relativism when doing business globally. Knowledge of what constitutes one's core beliefs and the role they play in the success of the enterprise undertaken will help avoid that pitfall. Sticking to core beliefs in the face of local opposition might look like short-changing oneself. But in the long run that always makes good business sense.

When Indian pharmaceutical companies started mushrooming after the Indian Patent Act of 1970 was passed, they demonstrated a knack for cutting corners in order to undercut the more well-established multinational companies (MNCs). Bribing doctors to buy prescriptions was one method employed. MNCs, known to maintain high standards of ethics and professionalism, soon joined the race. Today there is widespread activism and government crackdowns on these practices and MNCs can no longer claim the moral high ground. As a result, they have lost what used to be a unique selling proposition in attracting customers and professional talent.

Some values like precision, egalitarianism, diversity, and humanism are worth holding onto even when doing business across cultures. Most cultures respect and reward some form of these values and the differences are often in how rather than what.

Sellers should:

- Identify or reaffirm the core values of the company, service, or product.

- Ask: "How do the core values differ from the peripheral ones?" For example, for a car manufacturer, passenger safety and precision engineering would be core values because they ensure that passengers stay safe and cars don't break down. Passenger comfort might be a peripheral value, as not all cultures demand comfort while driving.

- Ask: "What are the areas where conflicts may arise on account of differing values?"

- Ask: "How might these conflicts be resolved?" This might demand a compromise and can be tricky. Take gender for example. Many South Asian cultures may strongly enforce gender roles even in the corporate sphere. Does a company that values egalitarianism object to perceived injustice or simply choose to accept it?

Watch for clues from the client on managing conflict. For some countries, harmony is the most important thing. They do not hit tough topics head on verbally. Watch for verbal nuances and body language.

The Difference Between Culture and Personality

There is a fine line between cultural sensitivity and cultural stereotyping. Remember that culture describes a group of individuals, and personality describes the individual. Behavioral manifestations of cultural tendencies take place through filters of personality, economic background, education, and experience. Just because a country scores low on power distance in its culture, does not mean everyone you meet there will take kindly to backslapping bonhomie.

At best, knowledge of cultural mores can help one avoid more egregious faux pas, especially in a group setting. In India, for example, including a vegetarian menu at any social function involving food is an absolute must. However, assuming that everyone avoids meat is equally false.

Once aware about cultural themes that are particularly sensitive in nature, when it comes to individuals, the best thing to do is ask. Make it clear that you come from a different cultural setting, that you are aware of the cultural importance of a particular action, and ask how the person in question would prefer that action be performed.

Managing time will vary in different countries. In America, it is common to make appointments and expect the schedule to go as planned. America and

Germany are two examples of being time focused versus being event focused. Showing up on time for appointments is important because time is seen as a precious commodity (time is money) and it is respectful to others to manage time well and in an organized, linear manner. Southern European and Arab countries take a different view of time. They are more event focused. For them the meeting or event is what is important, the precise starting time is less important. Many Asian cultures have an even different view—time is cyclical, as in the sun rising and setting daily for millions of years. It is not seen as a scarce commodity. Their view of time affects how they make decisions, careful and not in a hurry. Sales managers should be careful when planning their schedule globally—overscheduling can be a detriment; if one appointment goes long, it can mess up the rest of the day. When you are 20 minutes away from the next appointment it is easier to manage and reschedule.

Tips for Sellers

- Get to know your counterpart beforehand—a light back-and-forth over email or on the phone will be insightful prior to meeting in person.
- Stay aware and in tune to your customer during interactions. Watch for nonverbal feedback.
- When in doubt, ask.

Research and conversations with your trusted local contact will help when getting to know a new culture. A very important place sales managers can add value is by helping salespeople to view sales as educating the client versus just as persuading them to buy. Helping the client to identify their business issue and presenting a solution (or options) to solve that problem will lead to building credibility and trust.

Summing It Up

Culture is a lens through which people make sense of the world. Wearing another's lens or walking the proverbial mile in another's shoes will cause some discomfort at first, but those who master the process stand to reap huge gains.

Some businesses learn this the hard way. Like when Italian automaker Fiat entered the Indian market. Their promotions focused mainly on the superior engineering of their cars. Others, like Hyundai and Ford, embraced strong Indian values like family-based decision making. Their promotions adopted uniquely Indian slogans and were aimed at families rather than individuals.

Ford and Hyundai were rewarded with a thriving business in India, whereas Fiat was relegated to the bottom of the pyramid—a sad state of affairs for one of the world's finest car makers. As marketing and sales functions work together to understand values and cultures their country connection can be strengthened and improved.

Action Plan

- Assess the strengths of your team for cross-border selling. Create a development plan for those who need additional knowledge or skills on the topic.

- Leverage strong team members and other resources to share additional information. Share successful examples of culturally sensitive transactions in sales meetings to demonstrate the importance.

- Set up alignment meetings to ensure the existing sales process is consistent with how your company wants to do business with different countries. Recommend adjustments as needed to incorporate respect, sales cycle, local business acumen, and values.

References

"Dimensions." The Hofstede Centre. http://geert-hofstede.com/dimensions.html.

"International Sales Training – Developing a Cross-Cultural Sales Process." (2010). Tack International. www.tack.co.uk/blog/?tag=selling-to-different-cultures.

McClay, R. (2013). *111 Ideas to Engage Global Audiences*. Learniappe Publishing.

About the Authors

Anup Soans is the editor of *MedicinMan*, India's first magazine for field force excellence in pharmaceutical sales. He is the author of three books for pharma field force professionals and a facilitator of learning and development programs at India's top pharma companies. He conducts skill development and field force engagement programs that bring an alignment between employee aspirations and organizational objectives.

Joshua Soans has a master's degree in development studies from IIT Madras and is the executive editor of *MedicineMan*.

6
Managing Global Sales Teams

Claude Chadillon

Tim is a manager working for a large farm implement manufacturer in the Midwest. While visiting one of their international partners in England, he conducted a joint sales call with the lead territory sales representative and three-time top sales club winner, Andrew.

Tim began the meeting by introducing himself and showcasing the latest and most innovative benefits of their products. Throughout the call, Tim and Andrew seemed very misaligned. Phillip, the purchaser at a major distributor, seemed disinterested and preoccupied. Fifteen minutes into the call, Phillip excused himself and requested that the meeting be rescheduled to a later date.

During the call debrief, Tim surmised that Phillip must have had a "personal situation" and that it was simply a bad day for him to meet.

- Does this scenario seem familiar?
- How could Tim and Andrew have made the most of this call?
- What elements should they have considered for a successful call?

When managing internationally, sales leaders need to be aware of cultural aspects that affect the sale and should prepare their sales reps accordingly. When doing business globally, do your homework to understand the environment you will be working in. Be aware of:

- cultural differences
- communication styles and preferences
- meeting etiquette
- team alignment.

In this particular case, Tim did not consider the differences between American and British cultures. He got down to business the same way he would have in his local environment. Had he done his homework, he would have understood that the English business environment includes proper introductions, elements of dry humor, personal small talk (without emotion), and discussion of customer concerns. For British customers, building rapport is valued and a sign of respect. By not following the proper introduction, Tim created an uncomfortable environment and disregarded his customer's needs.

Do Your Homework

Proper cultural preparation is the key to success in any international business meeting. Sources of information about cultural differences include: a phone conference with the local HR representative or a member of the management community, the Internet, and books about cultural diversity. One book that I refer to frequently is *When Cultures Collide*, by Richard D. Lewis.

Before one of my trips to England I read the chapter about how the British interact in business meetings. I learned they take initial business meetings very seriously and begin on a last name basis. Soon after, jackets and ties come off and they use first names on second and third meetings. This helped me understand how to act during first, and subsequent, meetings with business partners. Although the British take business seriously they also value humor in a business interaction. Being prepared for dry and sarcastic humor really helped me to create a bond with our business partner. It was also useful with some of our staff and customers in Great Britain.

The book also shares thoughts and concrete tips on what behaviors to adopt when selling in other cultures. With the British, being sentimental or emotional has no place in a public or business environment. Talking too much is also often taken the wrong way. Taking sides and giving opinions is viewed as unprofessional.

Brits tend to simply look the other way, or go with another partner, instead of complaining or bringing forth their concerns in business situations. Therefore, you have to ask a lot of questions to get at the concerns and once you do, you must deal with them in an emotionless way.

In the opening example, if Tim had done proper research he could have avoided upsetting an important customer.

When preparing for any international business meeting, make sure you understand proper business introductions, what a particular culture values, and how to interact with sales subordinates. Involving the local leadership and representatives will increase enthusiasm and heighten the professionalism when facing customers.

Connect With Team Members

Engaged team members who are eager to participate are the most important element for global team success. To increase the effectiveness of a global team, enable members to communicate—both informally with each other, and more formally during team meetings. Use whatever tools your organization has to create a shared virtual workspace—one with a regular pattern of communication (scheduled virtual meetings, informal sharing of various topics and best practices) to promote the exchange of cultural information and other team topics. Create a set of standards and rules for using this common workspace. It's also important to set communication guidelines about what is acceptable to share and discuss.

Obviously one of the challenges for team meetings will be time zone differences. To overcome this obstacle, vary the schedules weekly or monthly to give everyone a turn to join at a reasonable time of day. Include the time zone on meeting invites to help avoid confusion.

A good practice is to document team meetings. Meeting minutes and follow-up communication should summarize the main points discussed, emphasize the decision points, outline the responsibilities moving forward, allow attendees to share additional comments, and verify understanding of the outcome of these meetings.

Make sure that language does not become a barrier to effective communication. If an official business language is used in your organization, be sure to follow the rules below.

Business Language Rules

- Make sure that language training is available to those who are non-native speakers.
- Promote the use of the official language at every possible occasion.
- Provide a list of officially used terminology to all team members.
- When conducting meetings or customer visits, be aware of your pronunciation and enunciation and make sure you are speaking clearly.

Get Aligned

To stay in sync with global team members, hold an alignment meeting each month and schedule face-to-face meetings whenever possible. Priorities of the monthly alignment meeting should include topics such as:

- local business priorities
- employee development status
- overall performance
- issues and concerns requiring support.

It's imperative that business priority alignment takes place on every conference call, meeting, or face-to-face interaction. Unclear objectives will create confusion and misalignment of focus. A global team can easily become disoriented and unmotivated if they get the sense that the organization is struggling to align priorities.

Commitment to the organizational priorities and goals will vary based on the individual perception of "What's in it for me?" It's important for the manager to communicate the value of the goals in a way that relates it to both the team's long-term vision and individual growth goals. If team members lack commitment they will focus their energy on areas that bring personal value.

A global team provides many benefits. Having access to team members 24 hours a day allows you to create a productive project environment and leverage a variety of experiences and skills for customer interactions. Requests for information at the end of a work day in Toronto can be forwarded to European counterparts and responded to by the start of the next working day.

Analyzing opportunities and isolating the right ones for the right audience is paramount to any global team. To do this, I usually hold a group session designed to identify the best practices and to eliminate the ineffective ones. To practice, we look at what works and we want to keep. We also look at what doesn't work that we want to either improve or stop.

Once opportunities have been prioritized and best practices identified, determine as a team how to implement the best course of action. Desired skills to achieve these best practices also need to be identified and training may need to be provided. This exercise allows you to build a library of behaviors and skills desired for your team. From this list, you need to determine how to best acquire the skills and habits. Team members benefit from this exercise by looking at their own work habits and skills and challenging themselves to limit the ineffective traits and adopt new ones that have been proven to work.

When planning training for team members, getting input from the team will not only provide a great product but will also provide instant buy-in and reduce any resistance to implementation. The team members will be the best catalysts to influence others to implement the solutions.

Choosing Your Global Team

Choosing global team members wisely is a must for a high-performing team. There are a number of factors that should be considered when choosing your team members. One key trait to look for is whether or not the personal values of team members align with the company's values. Skills and performance can be coached and tracked, but values are lived and cannot be taught, when values are part of company culture it is paramount that these align. It's also important that team members have a very high level of autonomy and the ability to work through issues. For example, remote workers can easily fall into an isolation syndrome, a pattern where people feel that they are working in a silo by themselves with little or no support. Allowing team members to fall into this pattern will create underperforming individuals and promote working toward one's own initiatives and directions instead of the team goals. Other characteristics to look for in global team members are autonomy, drive, competitive nature, vision, resourcefulness, and the ability to perform with limited guidance and supervision. Identifying these skills when hiring will improve success and limit the amount of work required to manage team members remotely. Using behavioral questioning—questions that ask candidates to describe how they have handled previous situations—is a great way to help you find the right global team members. Ask questions such as:

- What was your specific role in a successful business situation?
- How did you respond to a customer complaint?
- Please describe your behavior in the last big customer call.
- How did you handle your last customer objection?

Onboarding New Team Members

Onboarding new salespeople is crucial for any team—particularly for geographically dispersed sales team members. Setting the stage properly will provide direction and clarity of the expectations for the role. Formalizing the onboarding process will provide a way to monitor progress, outline desired behaviors, and create an action plan that will be agreed on by both team member and team leader.

Onboarding is the time to communicate the basics, such as parameters to live by, expectations of the role, company culture, team leader expectations, and legal and compliance rules.

In addition to providing yourself as a resource, a great onboarding practice is to assign a peer mentor to spend time with the new team member to help them get up to speed more quickly. If you are onboarding a new international team member and feel he may lack a bit of local support, assign someone who is local or as geographically close as possible. It is sometimes difficult for new team members to express concerns or even to share weakness with their team leader, so someone who has been around and knows how to get things done can relate to the struggles a new team member may feel.

During the onboarding process, sometimes new team members find themselves second-guessing their decision to join the organization. Provide them with clear and precise directions and communicate expectations and parameters. With a good onboarding process the time to performance will be reduced and productivity increased. As a manager, be available to manage that shift and their commitment to the organization. You may need to increase your support and be more available. As the new team member becomes more proficient, more knowledgeable of the organization and the customer base, and knows the resources available, you can start taking a bit more of a backseat. At this point, be more of a consulting resource, letting team members make decisions and venture out of the box now that they have a better idea of the organization and the parameters in place. Let them manage their business their own way while spot checking and building trust. Remember, team members who are fully onboard and performing well can become good mentors to others.

Ongoing Development

Whether you are working with high-potential or career salespeople or new team members, everyone needs a development plan. I use a contract of self-development with each team member. This is particularly important for salespeople, because gaining effectiveness can directly relate to accomplishing sales goals. We start with one, two, or three skills or behaviors to work on. In addition, we describe how that behavior will benefit the team or customer. It is important to understand why the skill or behavior is relevant, and for both parties to agree on what the manager will do and what the team member will do for the development plan. It is important for new team members to understand that you will be contacting them regularly to review their progress. Allow four weeks between reviews and book an hour or two to review the action steps taken on the plan. You are looking for evidence of actions and improvements. This might be walking through action steps taken, or walking through a report to demonstrate understanding of report analysis. When you meet, review the contract and have a dialogue about progress on the development plan. This should be a living and breathing document. After skills on the plan have been achieved, your team member should choose other skills or areas for development.

You should assess the development level of team members in that skill or topic area every time a new topic is covered. Frequent follow up and reassessment of the desired behaviors is a must for efficient onboarding and successful performance. Recognition of achievement will also support the development of new team members. Keep motivation to perform high by challenging team members with new initiatives, new project work, or mentoring other team members.

I found that one of our salespeople needed help with closing and listening skills. We put together a plan and I assigned training modules around closing and up-selling. We did role plays over the phone, and at times I played hard ball in order to see how she would handle it. I also asked her to document five calls. The salesperson walked me through each customer call including her positive opening, how she applied listening to understand customer needs, how she asked for the order or further commitment, and how she closed the call. Once this sales rep mastered these elements of the call, we updated her development plan and added other skills to work on.

Managing Life in the Fast Lane

When managing internationally, you have to be very careful with how you manage your time. This is clearly not a 9-to-5 job because it spans several time zones. Consider this job like a project and plan your time accordingly. Allocate a certain amount of time for each sales opportunity, daily tasks, team meetings, and travel. Try to stay true to this allocation so you can have time for family, friends, and your health. Achieving a balance between work and your personal life is extremely important. Too much work and not enough personal time will have a negative impact on your effectiveness as a manager.

Building Cultural Acceptance

David Livermore, of the Cultural Intelligence Center, developed some key characteristics of a culturally intelligent organization. While it was developed for an organization, the principles are valuable for a sales team as well.

- Trust: While trust is built intuitively between people with similar backgrounds, it takes consistent follow through and reliability to build trust in a multicultural setting.

- Engagement: When different perspectives are valued, people are more willing to speak up and offer ideas and opinions. Knowing what motivates people makes it easier to get their best work.

- Influence: Influence can happen with clients, and inside the organization with peers and even supervisors.

- Authenticity: Encouraging people to be themselves, even while learning to adapt required behaviors, will require less energy and will be less draining.

- Positive intent: When we do something like answer a call in a movie, we know it is because it is important. When others do it, we assume they are being rude. Assuming the best of people, even those who are different from us, can stop us from making harsh judgments.

Time Zones

Another thing to understand and plan for is time zones. Managing across time zones adds complexity. Make sure you reach out using email versus phone calls during team members' off hours. Schedule phone calls in advance so people are available and can answer your calls without interrupting their meetings or customer calls.

For example, if you are based out of Zurich and you manage people in the Americas and Asia, you are looking at both ends of the time spectrum. Time zones make it difficult to have discussions with both groups at the same time of day. If you have team members who don't mind working outside regular work hours, you can find times early morning and late evening to talk to both. Be sure to alternate meeting times so the same group isn't always meeting early or late. It is important to have everyone participate but you also need to be aware of their work schedules.

Priorities

Because there are always too many things to do and not enough time to do them all, I use the Eisenhower Matrix to categorize tasks and workload into four quadrants. Unless you are proactive and deliberate, you will find yourself playing catch up all the time. Here's how I use it:

- For important and not urgent, allocate time to get these tasks completed soon or they will become urgent. (These are "B-Tasks.")

- For items that are not important and are urgent, it is helpful if you can delegate these. (These are "C-Tasks.")

- Unimportant and not urgent tasks I call "dump it," or "tasks for dustbin." Spend time on more important things.

Figure 6.1

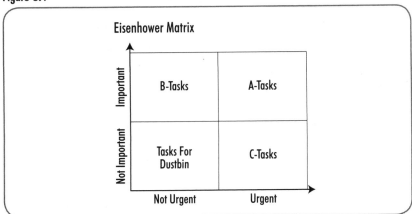

85

Email is another task that can take a lot of time. Allocate a certain time of day that you are effective and productive at completing emails. For me, it is the morning hours. If I have an hour or two early in the morning, I categorize my messages address the important ones first, and delegate tasks as necessary.

Travel

Managing globally requires a lot of travel. Schedule your trips in advance whenever possible. I typically plan a three- to four-month calendar and allocate family time in between trips. Planning a good quality family weekend is important. I get caught up on projects and emails during the week so I do not have to spend the family time on work.

Availability

Some countries work on Saturday or Sunday, so you may have to work on weekends. Plan for it. When you are not available, use an out of office notification to let people know that you are out. If you take time off, be sure to set up a key person others can contact when you are on holiday. Sometimes when you are not available, emergencies or urgent questions that need to be answered come up. Be sure your team is always supported by knowing when you are available and when you aren't. When you aren't available, make sure your team knows who they can contact to complete proposals and close business.

Summing It Up

Global management is exciting and there is always something new to learn. But as exciting as it is, it's often very demanding and requires different skills and a different focus than managing a co-located team. You may go through the same things—onboarding, developing skills, coaching, communicating—but the way you do these things is different because you are not all together in the same place. Managing across time zones, dealing with other cultures, and working with people that you don't see face-to-face on a regular basis can be challenging. To get a handle on these factors, do your homework. Find out about the different cultures you will be dealing with—read books and talk to people who are familiar with the cultures. Understand what time zones your team members are in and know what skills and talents each possess. Make opportunities for them to communicate with each other and with you.

Many people are competing for your time, all the time and at different times of the day and night. You need good management skills and the ability to prioritize and set boundaries. One priority should be making time for team members and supporting them in whatever they need to do their jobs. Another priority should be to yourself. Work to balance effectiveness with efficiency, team time with individual time, and management responsibility with leisure time. Achieving this balance can make your role as a manager of a global team both exciting and rewarding.

Action Plan

Questions for reflection:
- Do I manage people equitably, making sure their needs are met and they feel supported?
- Do I approach my work from a project perspective, proactively planning in order to spend my time on the right areas?
- Am I giving my family and loved ones the attention they deserve? Am I totally present when I am with them?
- Am I proactively planning my calendar in order to accomplish the most important things and drive business?

References

Lewis, R.D. (2005). *When Cultures Collide.* Boston: Nicholas Brealey International.

About the Author

Claude Chadillon has worked his way up from sales positions to sales leadership to director of global sales training and development with Hilti. He is responsible for the learning transfer of sales and leadership skills of 20,000 employees in more than 120 countries. He develops and delivers training around the world and lives the global trainer life. He was an APEX Best Portfolio Award of Excellence Winner in 2011.

7
The Sales Manager's Role in Training

Sandy Stricker

Does this scenario sound familiar? A salesperson isn't performing. He doesn't get many second appointments (if he even gets in the door the first time), he struggles with articulating the value your solution provides, and of course he isn't meeting his quota. The problem is obvious—he hasn't been properly trained. You think, "I'll send him to training, they can fix it." You enroll the person in class, he goes through all the skills that he's already had training on, and he goes back to doing the same old, same old. Three months later the salesperson is still having the same problems. You end up having to let him go, saying, "I felt bad but the training just wasn't working."

Time and time again, when employees fail to perform up to expectations after training, managers cite training's role in the problem. The training was too long, too short, too many role plays, not enough practice, didn't cover the right expectations, covered too many expectations, and a host of other shortcomings. But in truth, training alone is never the sole factor in bringing about improved performance, and is often not even the largest contributor.

In most scenarios, it's not that the training is poorly written or delivered or that the learner just doesn't have the capacity to learn. It's that the participant didn't get the support before training or understand the business reason for attending. During training, he may have had to attend meetings and return phone calls, which meant missing huge chunks of the learning. And when he returned to the job, instead of being asked about the training, he was welcomed back to a slew of emails, voicemails, and other urgent issues. Soon, the training program is long forgotten and the employee's manager is talking about how poor the training program is.

Why is this so? Why don't employees understand that the training they're about to attend is so important to their success? Ask a participant why he is in training and the answer is often, "Because my manager told me to come." But ask why his manager feels this particular training is of value, he typically can't answer. Why? Because the manager doesn't know what the training covers, what the outcomes are, or what the value of the training is. The manager sends someone to training because that topic "sounds" like it will fix a problem, or because there is an arbitrary number of training hours that each employee is supposed to take each year.

Why Is a Manager a Key Player in the Success of Training?

There are a number of factors that contribute to the success of training, and there are several books on evaluation and ROI that can help the training department isolate those factors. But the bottom line is that most of the other factors boil down to one thing—manager support.

This purpose of this chapter is not to blame managers for ineffective training results. I am a manager, and I understand how demanding the job can be. The purpose is to help you understand the important role you play in supporting learning and to give you knowledge and skills you can use immediately to help your salespeople get the most out of their training.

Training has costs associated with it, both money and time, and should be treated like an investment. As a business person, you want a return on that investment. Your organization wouldn't purchase equipment and then not do anything with it, would it? Well the same should be said of training. Whether it's external training with an actual dollar figure attached to it—or internal, which has time and effort costs—you want to make sure it's put to good use and not wasted.

Another reason to care is because it has an impact on your reputation as a leader and your success. As a manager, your employees look to you for guidance and direction. If you are supportive of training, and show that you believe in the value, so will your employees. In return, they will be more engaged during the training program, learn more, be able to apply the learning more effectively when they return, and be more successful selling.

Still not convinced? Research has shown two things over and over: the number one reason employees give for leaving a company is lack of growth and development opportunities; and employees don't leave companies, they leave managers. If you're not actively engaged in your employee's growth and development, chances are it won't be long before you're looking to fill their open position.

Finally, there's a huge payoff for you as the manager for being supportive of your employee's growth and development. The more you focus on and support their learning, the more engaged they become. You'll get a reputation as a manager that people want to work for because you are someone who cares about their employees' future. You'll also be recognized by your bosses as someone who's committed to helping the company grow, and that's good for your future.

Why Aren't Managers More Involved?

Most managers want to be involved in learning and want to be supportive, so why aren't we? In today's world, with reduced workforces and employees being asked to do more with less, managers are stretched thin and hope training can alleviate some of the burden of managing their associate's performance. But what they fail to realize is that a small time investment before and after the training can help drive performance and help the learning "stick."

I know you're busy. You have quotas to manage, paperwork, and administrative burdens to deal with. Where do you find the time to do the training department's job with everything else on your plate? Here's a tip—it's not the training department's job to develop your salesforce. It's their job to partner with you do develop your salesforce. The good news is that it's really not that hard to partner with training professionals to support your employees.

The biggest emphasis should be placed on what happens before and after training. Why? Because these are the points where you have the most influence and control. When your employee is in training, you have to trust that the training organization is doing its job by developing an outstanding program, which is delivered by skilled and competent facilitators. Before that training begins and once your employee returns, are the times when you can make the biggest difference in their learning by partnering with your training organization.

Four Easy Steps to Drive Learning

1. Start with yourself.
2. Prepare your salesperson for the training.
3. Support the employee during training.
4. Engage the employee after the training.

Start With Yourself

Make sure you understand the business outcomes and the "What's in it for me?" (WIIFM). Before you send an employee to training or approve his training request, make sure you understand what the training program is designed to do and how it will impact the business. How will it affect sales? What's in it for the participant? Will the training program give him the ability to identify more prospects in their territory? Gain more appointments? Give him the tools he needs to sell more widgets?

To answer these questions, your training department should be able to provide you with two important pieces of information: the objectives of the training and the agenda. The learning objectives tell you what the employee will learn as a result of successfully completing the training program. (And by the way, successfully completing the training means he has attended all portions and completed any pre- and post-training assignments. You can't expect an employee to have met the objectives if he spent half the time on the phone putting out fires.) This type of objective is good to know because it tells you what they should know when they return.

But learning doesn't mean much if the employees can't do anything with it. I learned statistical analysis in graduate school. I know I learned it because I have a piece of paper that says I received an A. But please don't ask me to calculate a standard deviation because I can't. There was no reinforcement, coaching, or guidance after the class.

What's of even more importance are performance objectives. This is what the employees should be able to do after successfully completing the training. This is where the rubber meets the road. A learning objective might read something like this: After successfully completing this program, the participants will be able to match the prospective buyer's style with an appropriate selling style. The performance objective might say they'll be able to sell to all four buyer types. As a manager, that's much more important.

You'll also want to look at the salesperson's current talents and skills and compare them to the objectives to determine if this is the right training. For example, if a performance objective is to be able to successfully describe the value your solution brings to a prospect's business, and you know for a fact this salesperson is truly a champion in those skills, you might consider a different training opportunity. If you have a salesperson who is really struggling with that skill, then you have the right training.

What if you have someone who already has that skill, but there are other things covered in the class? You might encourage your employee to focus on the additional learning he can take away and to look for any tweaks he might find to skills he already has.

The agenda tells you what will actually be done or covered in the training. This comes in handy as a starting point for the first conversation with your employee. You'll be able to talk about what he'll be doing in the training program and how it compares to his needs and the needs of the organization. The agenda is especially helpful if it shows role plays, activities, or action planning. Those are items that you'll want to talk about with your salesperson after the training program is finished.

Prepare Your Salesperson for the Training

Prior to the training program, set aside time to meet with your salesperson to discuss what's covered in training and why you both feel this is a worthwhile use of time. Discuss what the expected outcomes are, and how the training will benefit you, the employee, and the organization. Review the objectives with your salesperson. Ask him to articulate what he hopes to do differently when he returns and how it will help him sell more. Don't just tell him what he should do differently. Then it becomes your training, not his. You want to share your two expectations: what you'll be looking for after training, and your expectation that he participates completely in the training. The discussion should include how the employee will be able to practice and reinforce learning, how you'll measure success (for example, whether or not his performance has changed), and how you'll reward improvements.

Review any pre-work and make sure that your employee has completed it prior to the class start. Be sure to look closely at the pre-work. Often, your training department will have pre-class activities that include you. For example, the training may require a 360-degree assessment. Don't leave those pre-class assignments until the last minute and make sure your employee doesn't either.

The one thing most managers neglect to think about is clearing a path for the employee to be successful. This means working with him to ensure his calendar is as clear as possible and that someone is designated as a backup. Of course it's important for prospects and clients to be able to reach the salesperson—that's why someone should be a backup for urgent issues that may come up. This will allow your employee to focus on learning how to be more effective and not worry about what's happening back in the office. So often I see people eager to learn something new that will make them more successful, only to have them completely frustrated by the end of the training because they missed most of it dealing with urgent issues. If they really do have a lot on their plates, consider whether this is the best time to attend training.

Finally, before they embark on their training journey, schedule time with them to connect when they're finished. This is not, "Let's catch up when you're done with training." This is an appointment on the calendar that you both commit to with the main goal of debriefing the learning and discussing next steps. Arrange to meet with your employee as soon as possible (and at least within 10 days) after he returns to discuss his experience.

Support the Employee During Training

While the employee is in training, you can relax a bit. They are now in the very capable hands of your training organization. You can trust that you've prepared your salesperson for the training and that he's learning some very valuable skills to allow him to sell more.

But notice I said you'd only be relaxing a bit. The most important thing you can do now is to continue to clear a path for him to learn. This means running interference if needed and ensuring he's not being constantly interrupted by things that can truly wait. My motto is that unless a client or prospect is at risk, it can wait. Now certainly if the training is multiple days, there should be a game plan to determine how to handle situations, but the fewer interruptions the better. I understand that time in class is time not selling, but you want to make sure your employee is able to make the most of his time in the training.

Engage After Training

The training program is over and your salesperson is back in the office. Remember that meeting you scheduled for when he returns? Well now it's time to debrief the training and talk about next steps. This is not the time to have the employee come back to the office and do nothing with the training. Neglecting this follow up increases the chance any takeaways from the training will become a binder on the top shelf never to be looked at again.

I remember a sales manager who went through an extensive five-day training course on how to coach. At the end of the training she was excited to try out her newfound skills and make an impact. She returned to an inbox full of emails, a full voice mailbox, and a manager who didn't ask a single question about the training and instead launched into the craziness that had ensued while she was "away enjoying the donuts at training." The result? The job aids she had used so intensely in training were put on a shelf. Without practice, support, or coaching she'd forgotten everything she'd learned within three months.

The goal is to have a conversation with the employee and review what he learned and how he will apply the learning. In addition, depending on what the topic was, you might continue their learning with role plays, practice, and coaching. Some simple debriefing questions to get you started on this conversation are:

- Tell me about the training.
- What did you like about it? Dislike?
- What were some of the surprises?
- What did you learn that is different from what you knew or is different from how we do things here?
- What were some of the most important things you learned?
- How do you plan on applying those things?

If the course had an action plan, ask him to show it to you so that you can work together to develop a strategy to make that action plan happen. You may consider role playing, stretch assignments, or other activities to help cement the learning.

If you're going to role play with your employee, make it very specific to the training objectives. For example, if one of the objectives was to "get an appointment with a prospect on the first call," ask your salesperson to role play the phone call he would make to get that appointment. First, have him identify a real prospect he is hoping to get in to see and have him explain the strategy for opening the call. Give feedback and suggestions on how he might do this differently. Then, actually role play the conversation, with you playing the part of the prospect. Be tough but realistic. Your goal is to give feedback and to coach and guide your employee. This will boost his confidence and make him more open to the feedback.

Once the role play is done, ask the employee to conduct a self-assessment. What did he do well and what could he have done better? Most people will focus on the negatives, or what they "did wrong." Get him to focus on the positive. While you want him to see where the opportunities are, you also want him to see what he did right and encourage him to continue to use those skills.

Use a model such as "likes, concerns, and suggestions" to give feedback. In this model, you tell the salesperson what you liked about what he did, you share concerns about what he did, and then offer a suggestion for improvement.

Finally, work with your salesperson to develop a 30-60-90 day game plan. Your post-training conversation shouldn't just be a one-time event. You want to make sure that you continue to reinforce and support the employee until you've seen evidence that he's incorporated the learning into his day-to-day activities.

Supporting employees as they go through training shouldn't be considered "something else" for you to do. At the beginning of this chapter you read about the importance of employee development. You should make this part of the development you do daily. You're more than likely already having regular conversations with your employees. The pre-training conversation can be done as part of a regular one-on-one meeting. The post-training meeting should be a separate meeting, but can also be considered a developmental meeting. And as you're determining stretch assignments, consider tasks that can be part of the employee's development plan that is an area of focus.

What About E-Learning and Webinars?

Throughout this chapter, the focus has been on face-to-face training. But what if the training is an e-learning course or virtual training? Well the good news is it's all the same. You still want to follow the steps outlined in this chapter. It's still important that you understand what the training will cover, discuss the training and expectations with the employee, clear a path for them to be successful during the training, and then talk with them when they're finished. Follow this approach even if it's a 30-minute e-learning course. You just may not need to spend as much time in the discussions since the content and concepts are shorter.

Summing It Up

Whether your salespeople are attending a week-long training class, or sitting down to complete an e-learning module, consider it an investment of your organization's resources that needs to be followed up on. You just spent your time to read a number of tips to help maximize that investment. Don't let your time investment in this go unrealized. Your next step is to think about upcoming training your salespeople might have and to schedule that pre-training conversation with them.

Action Plan

- Set up follow-up appointments with your people to review and discuss any training they have taken in the past three months.
- Share your view of training and your general expectations at an upcoming meeting to let your team know you value it.
- Create a training reinforcement document that includes setting your expectations before attending and follow-up questions to ask after.

References

Brinkerhoff, R.O. (2006). *Telling Training's Story*. San Francisco: Berrett-Koehler.

About the Author

Sandy Stricker is the director of instructional design for the sales learning organization at Automatic Data Processing—one of the world's largest providers of HR business outsourcing solutions. She has been involved with learning and development for more than 15 years.

She's had a number of different roles in learning including leadership development, training and coaching, product training, service training, and now sales learning. Sandy's passions in learning and development include metrics and evaluations and identifying new ways to increase the value and impact that learning can bring to an organization. Her formal education includes a bachelor's degree in training and development from DePaul University, a master's degree in organizational behavior from Benedictine University, and she is currently working toward an MBA from Keller Graduate School.

8

Leveraging Your EQ for Sales Effectiveness

Lou Russell

Sales is a funny thing. One day, you're on top of the world, closing that big "whale" of a sale. The next week, you're down in the dumps because of a controversial price increase. It's a roller coaster world. The ability to be aware of and manage emotions is referred to as an emotional quotient (EQ). Many people know IQ (intelligence quotient). In sales and customer service environments, EQ is an important skill set to have.

Sales Skills for a Complex World

The world of making money has become very complicated. New technology, reduced sales support, global competition, business change, and international financial chaos have driven sales organizations to become leaner and more of a matrix. A lone sales manager can no longer do her job without the help of many others both on and outside her official sales team. These are people who don't really want to help, people who already have enough to do. As sales become more complex, working on each opportunity is more like a flash mob: random people coming together for short periods of time to do things that make some people happy and some people mad, and then disperse as quickly as they assembled. The bottom line: Your team is doing a lot more than working a prospect list.

"Flash mob sales" makes building brand and customer loyalty even more difficult. The deafening noise of the marketplace makes it very hard to differentiate yourself and be heard. More than ever, sales success requires:

- A clear value proposition for the market or customer. A clear, concise message is key to sales success.
- Listening, listening, listening, and checking for understanding. Bad news early (from the customer) is good news to you (so that you don't spend extra time and energy on deals that will go nowhere).
- Organizational skills to drive effective follow up and close the sale.
- Technology to drive less labor-intensive (expensive) customer relationship management (CRM) tasks.
- Infrastructure and people to ensure that one fulfilled sale will drive future sales.

Take a minute and give yourself some feedback on this list. Use the stoplight method: put a green, yellow, or red mark next to each bullet. What are the strengths of your team? What are their blind spots?

Now, think about how these bullets really occur in life. Each individual that you lead is working many leads and multitasking through many activities simultaneously, yet each needs a unique strategy that works specifically for them.

Meanwhile, your work life as their leader is also consumed by chaos and your own workload. How can you serve them in the chaos when you are in chaos as well? Jot down answers to some of these questions:

- What other factors are at play here?
- How can you serve your team better?
- How can you reduce this chaos?

It's likely that you, like most, are very frustrated with your current workload. Some of your big leads and existing customers who would like to buy again have been lost by something you or your team did not have time to do or did not do well. This drives frustration and stress. The growing frustration and stress drive mistakes. Stress can also drive inattention to detail and create rework. Subtle changes in your tone as you work with your team and your customers can change their perception of you. Refer to the following for an example of how that might play out.

Out of the blue, you get a call from someone about your products and services. This is from a very large company in your area. A former customer has recommended you.

As the sales manager, you immediately contact your best salesperson to set up a visit as soon as possible. No answer. The customer emails you a suggested date to meet and you call the same salesperson again—no answer. With no time to spare, you mentally pick the "next best" salesperson and call him, but he's on vacation. With a bit of trepidation you schedule your least experienced salesperson to go to the meeting with you because he answered the phone and is available.

You have a reasonably good meeting with the customer. Your salesperson is a few minutes late because you forgot to give him the new customer address. He also answered a few questions incorrectly but you corrected them quickly and you don't think the customer noticed.

It's time to submit a proposal. You know the new salesperson can't do this alone. It's a big proposal, and it means a lot of money. You create a draft and have the salesperson proof it.

An existing customer calls and is livid about the quality of the product they received. You spend an hour or more on damage control. That same day, one of your salespeople quits, and the work is dumped on you because everyone else is so overloaded. You miss your son's soccer game where he scored his first goal. As you are working late into the night, your frustration grows. "Am I the only one that can do things? Where's everybody else? Why do I get stuck with all this extra work?" You work yourself into a tired anger and quickly send an email to your boss with your frustrations.

The next morning, your boss asks you to come in. You're pretty tired and still unfocused. As you enter her office you can tell this is not going to be a happy meeting. She shares a paper copy of your email and asks what you were referring to. You struggle a bit to answer the question, not sure what to say. She mentions that the irate customer you were working with on the quality issues has expressed concerns that you and your team are not giving them the focus the customer needs. The conversation ends with you apologizing and becoming more stressed.

A week later, you realize that you have completely forgotten to finish up the proposal for the new potential business. You decide, due to lack of time, to send the proposal that was edited by your novice salesperson without looking at it again. You plan to call the customer later in the week but you don't remember. On Sunday evening as you work through your email you finally take a look at the proposal you sent. It has many typos and the numbers were mistakenly changed. On Monday you get an email that the customer is going with someone else.

What emotion would you be feeling if you were in this situation? What were the triggers? What mistakes and rework were created because of blind spots due to stress?

Figure 8.1

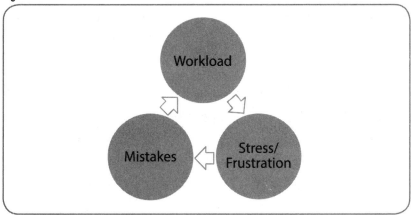

The story illustrates how emotions can create blind spots that prevent us from seeing the best way to deal with life's challenges. However, emotions are also a protective mechanism. They are a call to action from your brain to watch out for something that is trying to harm you. In the next section, you will learn why emotions are so important to your ability to lead effectively.

Stress, the Brain, and the Impact on Effectiveness

The reptilian brain is the most primitive part of your brain. Its job is to keep you alive. When the reptilian brain sees danger, it triggers an instant defense plan to save you quickly. Internal hormones fly automatically, and your heart rate and circulation increase so that your arms and legs are ready to fight or flee. Your eyesight focuses on the danger and nothing else. The frontal part of your brain, where if/then/else thinking resides, is shut down—there will be no time to think through the best solution. The pathway to your memories, deep in your neocortex, is temporarily detoured—no time to look anything up. Immediate danger requires an immediate response.

Unfortunately, your reptilian brain doesn't always know the difference between an actual threat and a diva salesperson upsetting the rest of the team. Both events may trigger similar negative emotions (fear, stress, frustration, anger, and so on).

The reptilian brain is a gradual reaction, depending on the perceived threats. When the reptilian brain provokes a significant enough emotional response, your brain ramps up quickly. It returns to a functional state very slowly. On average, a person will experience a lack of focus and blind spots for four hours after a significant negative emotional event. This blindness is prime space for errors that create the next day's rework and possibly another day of living by the dysfunctional imperative of the reptilian brain. I recently experienced a strong negative emotion when the bombs went off at the 2013 Boston Marathon and my brother was running near the finish line. Although we found out he was fine in a little under an hour, I was unfocused and dazed for 24 hours.

It's important to remember that negative emotions are not bad and they serve an important function. They are calls to action—both important and unimportant—and it's up to you to decide which. Pushing them away or pretending not to have negative emotions when appropriate is dysfunctional and will make you sick.

To function effectively in today's chaotic world requires two abilities, which together form emotional intelligence. These can be strengthened with practice that will help you avoid too many reptilian brain days.

Emotional Awareness and Emotional Regulation

Emotional awareness is the ability to recognize when a negative emotion is beginning to occur inside you, to correctly diagnose why it is occurring and to determine what the appropriate response is.

Once aware, emotional regulation is knowing how to calm yourself down if the emotional reaction is not appropriate to the situation (example, no coffee left versus tragic illness in your family). How you calm yourself depends on your unique values, behaviors, and wellness (sleep, nutrition, and so on), as well as the mental models that have been built throughout your life when bad things have happened. The following shows an example of two differing mental models for the same event.

Your boss has overloaded you with new standards and documentation for you to teach your team and all the other teams that aren't directly your responsibility.

One way of thinking about this (called a mental model) is that your boss is picking on you. This will likely trigger a negative emotion of anger, and the reptilian brain will engage the fight, flight, or freeze response. Any of these three options will make it more difficult for you to be successful with your additional workload and at an extreme, might cause career suicide.

A different mental model is that your boss thinks of you as the go-to person when things get rough. This will likely trigger a positive emotion of pride, which will empower you to work effectively on your additional workload, delegate well to others on your team, and improve your career success.

When appropriate, catching your brain before it gets to the fight, flight, or freeze stage helps you be at your optimum performance and be resilient and flexible. Not catching your brain in time guarantees rework, driven by careless mistakes that were caused by blind spots used by your brain to protect you.

This powerful statement merits another pass: You make a choice when negative emotions occur to either continue to regulate (fight to keep calm) or give in to fight, flight, or freeze. You decide. The stress you feel at work right now comes from your interpretation of events, not the actual events themselves.

What does fight, flight, or freeze look like in corporate America? Think about it and watch for it in your world. Here are some examples:

How do sales managers fight?

- Send a judgmental email and copy everyone to avoid having a difficult conversation with the one person who needs it.
- Confront someone loudly, especially in a public place.
- Ask questions to trip up a person in one of their meetings rather than deal with their performance issues privately.

How do sales managers take flight?

- Go off the grid. Use sick days, meetings, or hide in coffee shops with no explanation.
- Find people to socialize with instead of working, especially during happy hour.
- Avoid confronting or verbally participating in important meetings with individuals who need feedback.

How do sales managers freeze?

- Hide behind busy work, for example, deleting emails for hours on end.
- Get sick, take more days off.
- Go through the motions. Follow the letter of the law regarding the sales process but never really do what it takes to grow staff to close a sale.

In each case, these reactions to negative emotions are natural and logical to your brain. But they also take you further from where you want to be. You are not a victim of your brain unless you let yourself be. You have the power to mitigate these barriers to your success.

Strengths Are Also Weaknesses

You have a unique set of talents that no one else on earth has. You have behaviors that are easy for you and others that are very difficult. You have unique strengths that drive how you invest your energy in work, family, and life. Knowing your strengths and weaknesses is critical to regulating your emotions.

There are multiple assessment tools to measure your behavioral strengths. DISC is a very actionable choice. Figure 8.2 shows the four components of DISC. Each of us is a unique combination of all four.

Figure 8.2

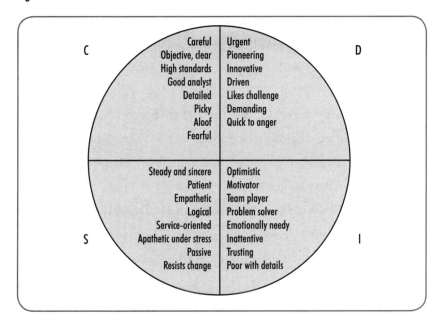

A simple diagram like this is helpful for understanding DISC and behavioral preferences, but is not adequate in clarifying what your particular strengths are. Starting at the top right quadrant, "D" stands for dominance. Someone with a high dominance will measure how successful their day is by asking this question: "Did I check off more tasks today than ever before?" A person with strong "D" behaviors is about tasks and speed. In addition, this person will:

- measure against himself or herself (not others)
- be blind to work that will not allow checking off tasks
- get angry if someone else prevents them from checking off tasks
- treat anger as a task—yell, then get over it.

Next, in the bottom right quadrant is "I" for influence. Someone with a high influence will measure how successful each day is by asking this question: "Did I convince more people than ever before to follow my lead? In doing so, did I also convince them that I am amazing?" A person with strong "I" behaviors is about people and speed. In addition, this person will:

- measure against others, vulnerable to the emotions of others
- be blind to work that will not allow evangelizing and getting positive attention
- get hurt if someone doesn't like him or her.

People who are successful at sales tend to have a DI behavioral preference. They like to move very quickly, evangelizing people (selling), and checking off new customers (closing). If you do not have this profile, it is still possible to be successful at sales, but it's going to be much harder for you and more exhausting.

Living in behavior styles that are not your natural styles is called adapting. Adapting is like wearing a heavy costume trying to be someone you are not. It can be exhausting and stressful, which triggers the reptilian brain. There are two types of adapting:

- consistently trying to be someone you are not to get along in the world you perceive you are in
- temporarily (for example, in a meeting) and mindfully adapting your behaviors to connect with a prospect or customer.

Sales managers and salespeople who can do the latter are more successful and healthier than those who use the first option.

A DI brain is stressed by the following triggers:

- slowness: boring meetings, endless conversations, slow speaking people (DI)
- being unable to check things off: lack of accountability from others, people who need too much information (D)
- being disliked or not being acknowledged: being talked down to, ignored, or insulted (I).

Regulation ideas that may work for a DI:

- a quick walk around the building
- doing something else that is easily completed (checked off) (D)
- remembering successes of the past, being with people who adore you (I).

It is powerful to work in your strengths and it is where you do your best work. It is also seductively easy to over use your strengths. A person with high "D" will tend to manifest multitasking manic behavior when stressed. A person with high "I" will tend to be ultra-sensitive to feedback when stressed. The strength easily becomes a weakness when overused.

As you can see, we've only done half the profile. The other two behaviors are equally important to sales professionals' emotions. Starting at the bottom left quadrant, "S" stands for steadiness. Someone with a high steadiness will measure how successful their day is by asking this question: "Did I carefully acknowledge every individual that I met today? Did I make their day better?" A person with strong "S" behaviors is about people (one at a time) and carefulness. In addition, this person will:

- measure against others' moods; be vulnerable to the emotions of others
- be blind to work that will potentially upset or hurt someone else's feelings
- remain calm and positive no matter how he or she feels inside.

Next, in the bottom right quadrant is "C" for compliance. Someone with a high compliance will measure how successful each day is by asking this question: "Did I get at least one task done perfectly (by my own secret measurement) or if I couldn't get it done perfectly, did I set up a diversion so I wouldn't have to finish it compromised?" A person with strong "C" behaviors is about tasks and perfection. In addition, this person will:

- measure the task against his or her own secret rules defining quality
- be blind to the needs of other people
- create diversion with a countenance of mistrust and doubt that makes others back off.

Here are two scenarios showing how these "S" and "C" profiles are critical to a DI salesperson to deliver on contracts successfully. A SC profile is common for middle managers with buying authority. You really need to be able to influence these people in your company or as customers, but your first reaction will be that they drive you crazy. Notice how D/S and I/C are opposites on the wheel and in focus, which drives a natural conflict.

Scenario 1: Talking With the Distribution Center

Your top customer calls you, angry because an important order has not arrived as planned. You calm him down (using your "I") and quickly dial the distribution center manager, Jo. You are pretty angry because this isn't the first time they've messed up important sales. Jo answers, as always with a pleasant hello. You respond with a quick, assertive tone and demand that this order ship overnight immediately. Jo pauses and starts to tell you about another account her team is committed to. You cut her off and make it perfectly clear that you are her priority or else. Jo pauses again and in the pause, you hang up.

Again, your top customer calls you the next day. The order did show up but it is incomplete. Once again, you call Jo. Jo calmly explains that she did the best she could do, but she did not have the parts. You demand to know why she didn't tell you that yesterday. She says that she tried to, but you seemed in a hurry and she knows you have very important people to keep track of. You hang up in frustration.

Knowing what you know about negative emotions and triggers, let's look at how productive these two discussions were in meeting the goals of the organization.

Table 8.1

Person	Behavioral Strength	Emotion	Trigger	Better Approach
You	DI	Frustration/ Anger	A checked-off task (sales contract) was unchecked	Seek first to understand versus fight. Listen carefully before jumping to conclusions and hanging up (flight).
Jo	S	Hurt, worried about you being angry	Conflict	Suggest a solution quickly and concisely instead of explaining why you can't (flight).

The critical thing to notice in this scenario is that each person is operating out of their strengths and is blind to the perspective of the other. They are both sane from their perspective, but combined they create insanity.

Scenario 2: Talking With the Legal Department

You get an idea for a wonderful email for each of your sales staff to send to all your prospects. Leveraging a popular television show, you ask one of your buddies to create a cartoon with your customers in the roles of the television show, all using your products. It's hilarious (I). You're positive you will be able to get this from concept to email delivered in less than 24 hours (D).

You get a voicemail message from Ray in the legal department that you need to call him immediately. From his tone, your read is that you have done something wrong but you have no idea what. Those legal guys are always looking for something to criticize (ID). You're completely unprepared for what he says.

Apparently, you have violated a copyright law with your use of the graphic and this has become a bigger problem because the cartoon has gone viral. Ray has all the facts and they prove you were wrong and acted too quickly, without thinking through the consequences of your idea. There has been a call from the television series' legal department. You apologize profusely (I), at the same time feeling stupid (D), but Ray doesn't show any emotion. You stumble out fuming about how ridiculous legal issues have become. You're in a deep emotional hangover for days, unable to deal with your customers until you snap out of it. You still don't really know what the long-term impact on your career will be.

Knowing what you know about negative emotions and triggers look at how productive these two discussions were in meeting the goals of the organization.

Table 8.2

Person	Behavioral Strength	Emotion	Trigger	Better Approach
You	DI	Inadequate/ Angry	You made a mistake that made other people see how flawed you really are. You are angry because the world is ridiculous.	Work on stopping yourself from implementing ideas before they are vetted appropriately. Emotionally own your mistakes and realize that you cannot be perfect (fight/ blame).
Ray	C	Anxious/ Fearful	The rules have been broken and they should never be broken.	Most mistakes can be forgiven with the right tone and approach. Build a collaborative solution to the immediate problem, including the salesperson, to learn how to avoid this in the future.

Again, each person is operating out of their strengths and is blind to the perspective of the other. Knowing each other's triggers can help people begin to value each other as resources for filling in the blind spots that we have, rather than positioning the other person as an adversary. Notice how the DISC strengths drive the triggers and also dictate how to regulate emotions, allowing a person to adapt temporarily to collaborate with someone who sees what you don't see. The pressure from the reptilian brain is both our purpose and our problem.

The Intervention (Not the Fix)

I once heard Sue Miller Hurst, originator of Starshine Foundation, say "If you think someone is a jerk, you look for ways their jerk-ness shows up." Growing your emotional muscle takes work, just like growing any other muscle. It starts with awareness of mental models and beliefs that you treat as fact in your own brain. These facts can create the trigger that leads to the stress-induced, emotional response. Unfortunately, there is no fix for this, especially a simple fix. Instead, you will need to intervene in multiple ways as you grow your awareness and regulation portfolio. Here are some tips that may work for you.

To grow your awareness:

- Watch another sales manager that you admire. How are they getting the results you want to get? What do you notice about the way he or she manages emotions?

- Describe your strengths and weaknesses to someone close to you and ask for clarification to improve your ability to self-assessment.

- Consider whether you have a realistic self-perception.

- Reflect on how your emotions have taken you from your goals in the past. What were the triggers?

- Keep a journal about your significant emotional responses to situations.

- Keep a list of your strengths and opportunities for improvement and read it daily.

- Think of where in the workplace you use your strengths and weaknesses.
- Create a challenging action plan to develop the areas you want to improve.

To grow your regulation:

- Practice self-restraint by listening first, pausing, and then responding.
- Learn to step away from difficult or overwhelming situations.
- Be committed to not interrupting others.
- When frustrated, summarize the situation to determine triggers.
- Plan effective responses to predictable, repeating situations.
- Determine what activities improve your mood and use them when you start to get stressed.
- Focus on events that provide calm or positive emotions.
- Keep a log of your self-management skills.
- Discuss ways of expressing emotions appropriately with your team.
- Put things in perspective. How will you feel about this in a week?

Other strategies to consider:

- The same stuff you know already—eat well, sleep, exercise, and avoid too much caffeine and alcohol. A stressed out body is more vulnerable and perceives more triggers as threats.
- Your brain and body seek consistency together. Think about how you would be sitting, or walking, or behaving if you were having the best day of your life. Now do those things. Your emotions may follow.
- Competition is the natural state for a DI sales professional. Collaboration is not the opposite of competition. Learn to collaborate to win. Work to see others in small, temporary adaptations.
- Clarify roles and processes. You are likely not a person who likes a lot of definitions and paperwork, but other people need boundaries to clarify the purpose of their role. Purpose is the best way to engage others.
- Drive accountability. Don't let the "I" side of your brain gloss over poor behavior and lack of delivery. Don't let the D side of your brain scream at people without getting the context of the poor behavior.

Instead, seek first to understand, and then reinforce the behavior you expect.

- Laugh and help others laugh. It's the great equalizer.

Awareness and regulation are important skills for a manager to learn to be effective working with others. Managers need to grow their own muscles before they will be effective helping their team do the same.

Summing It Up

Emotions are tools used by your brain to protect you and help you be successful. Fight, flight, or freeze are appropriate reactions when we are physically or emotionally in grave danger. Let run amok, emotions are inappropriate reactions that can trick us into a cycle of mistakes and rework driving more stress. The only thing that can grow your emotional muscle is you.

Sales and leadership positions often have a reputation for bossiness. Emotional success dictates a different approach. Enjoy this tale from Aesop's Fables as an example:

The north wind and the sun were arguing which was the stronger. On seeing a traveler they agreed a suitable test would be to strip him of his cloak. First the wind blew with all his might, but the more he blew, the more the man wrapped the cloak tightly around himself. When the sun's turn came, he gently beamed at the man, who loosened the cloak. The sun shone brighter still, and the man threw off his cloak.

Action Plan

For the manager:

Set a reminder on your phone for 3 p.m. every day for five work days in a row. When the alarm goes off, quickly note in a calendar entry on your phone your answers to the following:

- Name the emotion you are having right now.
- Rate the emotions intensity from 1 (Low) to 10 (High).
- List three things that are triggering that emotion in you.

On the sixth work day (likely a Monday), take 15 minutes to think about the following as you reflect on your entries for each of the five days prior:

- What do you notice about the emotions that you experienced each day? Were they similar or different? Why?
- If you experienced negative emotions, how did the emotion impact your work in terms of leading others, rework, or innovation?
- Reflect on the triggers that you experienced during the five days. What were the three things that you saw most often as a trigger to your negative emotions?
- For each of the three triggers that occurred most often, were you surprised? How do these reoccurring emotions detract from your ability to work effectively and/or live your personal life?
- Think about the energy cost of the negative emotions and how it impacted your productivity. How was your response not productive or appropriate?
- Redefine your thought process around the three triggers. How can you look at the trigger differently to maintain your emotional strength?

For the sales team members:

Use the following questions to discuss stress and sales effectiveness, one at each meeting:

- How does competition between salespeople hinder and encourage sales effectiveness? What could we do as a team to leverage both our competition and our collaboration more effectively to drive sales?
- Are there other internal organizations that the sales team has to work with that are stealing energy and causing stress? Which organization is the most difficult to collaborate with? Why? What can be done to improve that relationship to reduce stress?

About the Author

Lou Russell is the CEO/Queen of RMA, an executive consultant, speaker, and author whose passion is to grow companies by growing their people. Through speaking, training, and writing Lou draws on 30 years experience helping organizations achieve their full potential. She inspires improvement in leadership, project management, and individual learning using consulting and her seven practical books. Through humorous stories with on-the-ground experience you will be encouraged by Lou's upbeat style, and leave with the enthusiasm and tools to improve the bottom line. You will be moving, laughing, participating, inspired, and challenged. Most importantly to Lou, you will learn. For more information about the three-part Trimetrix EQ assessment please email info@russellmartin.com.

9
The Hiring Dilemma: Advice for Sales Leaders

Joseph Anzalone

In the seminal management tome *Good to Great*, Jim Collins compared leaders to bus drivers. The leader's top priority is to choose the right people for the bus: "if you have the wrong people on the bus, nothing else matters. You may be headed in the right direction, but you still won't achieve greatness. Great vision with mediocre people still produces mediocre results."

This is especially true for the sales leader. In this chapter, you will learn:

- "the three Ds"— key personality traits you should look for when hiring salespeople
- valuable tips for screening and interviewing
- the most common sales hiring problems and how to avoid them.

Common Hiring Scenarios

What happens when, despite our best intentions, we have the wrong people on the bus? Or if they're in the wrong seats? To best depict that common dilemma, let's check in with three fictional sales leaders. The issues that appear in these short stories may be familiar to you.

Blaire

Somewhere in a modern office park in the American northeast sits Blaire, a regional sales director. Her region's sales figures glow in front of her as she takes the last two sips from her afternoon cup of coffee the weekly sales team call fast approaching. She inherited a team of eight regional account executives, and has hired three more. They are specialists in outsourcing, approaching teams of purchasing directors and human resources managers about the cost and flexibility benefits of temporary and on-call workers to perform large-scale administrative and basic financial functions. Performance is down. After two quarters of sub-par performance, Blaire furrows her brow as she studies the declining, red figures on her monitor.

Most disturbingly, the three newest account executives—her choices—are the performing at the same level as those she's inherited. This reality, like her now lukewarm coffee, is tough to swallow. She believed from her previous experience that she had this hiring stuff down. She looked for highly educated, experienced, and competitive types with a natural taste for winning and simply turned them loose. HR seemed to be on board with her approach. She didn't understand what could be wrong.

One such thoroughbred, Kirsten, appears on her caller ID 10 minutes before the team call is to begin. After bringing over a couple of clients from her previous company, Kirsten has struggled to land new customers. Blaire sighs, tosses her coffee cup, and jabs a button in front of her.

"Hi Kirsten. Ready for the call?"

"Hi Blaire. Can we talk real quick?"

"Sure, what's up?"

"Well, you see my numbers. My appointments and presentations seem to be going great. I don't get it. I didn't want to bring this up in front of everyone else, but I don't think I can do this. I used to close three deals a week. I haven't produced a signed deal in two months!"

"Kirsten, you will. You're doing the activity, that's all it takes. Just trust the system. We'll get you back into training. Maybe you should practice our sales process again. I'll help you."

"I have been! What else should I do? What have I been missing? Is our marketing effective? Everyone is going through purchasing now. These e-auctions are killing me. I mean…you can't be happy either!"

"Well, let's talk after the call."

Rob

Three thousand miles away in Orange County, California, Rob, the director of sales at a recently renovated hotel known for its efficient service and excellent meetings facilities, sits in a spacious meeting room, his large frame straining to fit into a cushioned function chair. The staff bustles behind him, rolling in and unfolding additional tables and spreading crisp white linens, preparing the room for the next meeting. Across from him sits Sonja, his new assistant director of sales. Her face is flushed and red from crying. Rob, prone to blunt talk, steels himself for the conversation.

"Listen, Sonja, how long have we worked together? Nine years? You've always been a top performer here. The best front desk person we've ever had. The best sales assistant. Customers love you. I have no doubt you'll be a top performer again. You've gotta understand it's a numbers game. We've got all kinds of leads here. Follow up on them. Use your charm. Get out there and visit them if you have to. Who's gonna say no to you?"

"This is different!" Sonja wails. "These people don't want to talk to me! I call them, I email them, I have even texted them and they just want me to send them the rates. I mean what am I supposed to say? No?"

"That's just an objection!" says Rob, losing his rehearsed composure. "We talked about this in training. Remember? What do we say when a customer asks about rate? What do we say?"

Sonja looks up, coughs, and shakes her head slowly in response. Rob is nonplussed. He thought Sonja, the most popular person at the hotel, would be his best hire yet. Smart, polished, and diligent, he'd never seen her struggle, even handling the most difficult customer complaints. Rob takes a mental note to start looking for someone else. That new girl in catering, Emily, might be good.

Curtis

In the withering heat of West Texas, Curtis, an independent financial advisor and proud entrepreneur, sits comfortably in his office and reflects. He is having quite a day. Three appointments, three new clients, and it's not even time for lunch yet! His assistant, Brenda, strolls into his office after saying her goodbyes to Curtis's newest clients and gives him a knowing smirk.

"Don't get too comfortable. You've got five more lined up for today. When are you going to start slowing down?"

"Soon as Rory, that kid out there, starts picking it up," says Curtis in his Odessa drawl, looking distastefully through his thick office window at a slight, redheaded, bespectacled man in the next office, a phone headset clinging to his ear.

What is wrong with that kid? Curtis thinks. Maybe Brenda has an opinion. He knows she will give it to him straight; they've worked together for 28 years. "How's he doin' anyhow? It's been five months. He's gettin' all the leads I can't get to. Heck, when I was his age, I'd be doin' cartwheels with the leads he's gettin'!"

Brenda considers this. "Curt, how many new advisors have you hired in the past five years? Seven? Eight?"

"Somethin' like that."

"And how many are still here?"

"Yeah, yeah, I know, but I can't afford to pay no base salary, not with the turnover in this business. This should be easy enough. I take the large cases, they get the small ones—the ones I built my business on. Tell you what, they've got it a lot easier than I did when I started. Remember our first office?"

"Let's not go down that road again Curt," says Brenda. "The bottom line is you can't keep working this hard. You have to find someone else. And if you've had seven kids in here, and none of them are working out, what's the one thing they all have in common?"

"Ummm....they're lazy?"

Brenda chuckles. "No. You've found them all, and you've managed them all. You're the issue here. You can't just offer this job to every friend of your nephew, or every son of your client that needs a job. You're not just hiring another advisor here. This could be your legacy."

"Listen, Bren, half these kids went to SMU. Just like me," says Curtis, his voice rising. "But I could close half those leads with my eyes closed! Why can't they?"

Brenda looks at him like a parent considering her child, "Well, they're not you, are they?"

Beware the Myths

There is perhaps no new hire more fraught with unforeseen and inconsistent results than the salesperson. As illustrated in our three scenarios, the same issues can occur regardless of the industry, type of business, region of the country, or temperament of the leader.

Sometimes, the leader believes he understands the hiring profile based upon past experience, and the salesperson simply needs more training, as was the case with Blaire. Or, as in Rob's case, hiring decisions are based on the leader's firsthand knowledge of the candidate's superior performance in another, seemingly similar position, as we saw at the hotel. And in our small, entrepreneurial advisory business, Curtis is simply bewildered.

Our fictional sales leaders have fallen for a few of the myths about what makes a great salesperson. While identifying sales talent is often more art than science, it's wise not to fall prey to these tempting beliefs.

Myth Number One: Personality

Everyone has heard the same story at one time or another, from either their manager or senior leader, and it goes something like this: "See that top performer? Well, I found her in a restaurant, waiting tables. I knew she'd be great in sales, so I talked to her, gave her my card, and look at her now!" The logic, of course, is that you can find strong sales talent virtually anywhere—you just need the intuition to see it, and the gumption to approach it. Does this happen? Sure. Is it a hiring rule you should follow? Not really.

When looking for your next salesperson, realize there's a difference between someone's outgoing personality and what actually drives her. In our scenario we see Rob buy into this myth. He believes Sonja would have unlimited potential because customers love her and she loves them. Rob believes Sonja is adept at developing relationships, so he assumes that she would be eager to develop more relationships as a sales professional. Sonja, however, may have been driven by pleasing customers, not necessarily making sales. There is a big difference between the two. Moreover, this candidate type is often the strongest in interviews. They make excellent first and second impressions. This ability, while admirable, is often overrated by the hiring supervisor, especially in today's selling environment of longer selling cycles and multiple decision makers.

Myth Number Two: Experience

This can be tricky. Some of your candidates may indeed have experience, and perhaps they've even been successful in their previous sales positions. This factor, however, can also prove limiting. It is crucial to understand what their previous position demanded of them. Sales positions are highly diverse.

In our first scenario, Blaire hired Kirsten because of her track record of success in sales. Indeed, Kirsten could be an excellent salesperson in the right situation. But she is frustrated by the length of the selling cycle. Kirsten may have thrived in an environment with quicker, easier transactions that better suited her temperament. In her new role, the selling cycle is longer and the buying process is more complex. Kirsten, motivated by quicker successes, is already losing her patience and motivation. In the end, Blaire believes she's got a training problem. She doesn't. She has a hiring problem.

Yes, Kirsten brought a few clients with her, but eventually those previous relationships run out, and it's time to bring in new business. Blaire has made the additional mistake of assuming that would give Kirsten a jump start—something we used to call "hiring for the Rolodex." This strategy often backfires. The migrating customers may have been so easy for Kirsten to bring over that landing new ones only seems that much harder to her, further complicating the problem for Blaire.

Myth Number Three: Hire Someone Like You

This malady is found in all companies, industries, and sizes. Take our friend Curtis in the last scenario. He's a busy entrepreneur. He doesn't have time to consider the many nuances involved in finding the right person for his office. Instead, he makes a mental list of what he needs in a salesperson—a list that sounds a lot like him 30 years ago. Curtis is from Texas, went to SMU, and got into the business at 28 years old; now, his new sales hires all look suspiciously the same. The interviews with these candidates go quickly, the questions easy, the conversation lively and natural.

It's not uncommon for successful salespeople, now in a hiring position, to make this mistake. Like Curtis, they have been so effective partially because of their self-confidence and positive self-image. Subconsciously, their reasoning is this: "If the guy is like me, how can he go wrong?" Those attributes he valued, however, were not the ones that led to his own success.

Curtis, Blaire, and Rob may have been great salespeople. Now, however, they are leaders and hiring managers. The urgency, intuition, and confidence that made them successful salespeople is misguiding them as they try to identify, hire, and manage their talent.

Start With the Essential Traits

When identifying new talent, look for a verifiable track record on these three crucial characteristics, or "the three Ds":

1. Drive: Does the candidate have a history of completing every project they start? Or does she eagerly throw herself into new initiatives, only to let them languish during the execution phase? Your new sales professional should be able to tell you, in detail, how she brought sales initiatives and prospect meetings to completion. A good candidate will describe her thought process in sensible, clear, and convincing terms and you'll sense an inner drive and desire behind her responses. Her

drive will be evident in virtually everything she has done. Don't forget to probe into other, seemingly unrelated, accomplishments in her background. A pattern of success will emerge from the strong candidate.

2. Discipline: Virtually every strong salesperson has this trait in common. Their lives have been infused with self-discipline. No one has ever had to push them to focus on the necessary, valuable activities that lead to sales. Here, it is especially important to "read between the lines" of the candidate's resume. Did he make sales happen through a series of self-directed, disciplined actions, or was he the fortunate benefactor of an efficient system at his company? Did he build his own book of business, or inherit it? In other jobs or pursuits in his background, how much discipline was involved? If you can get satisfactory answers to these questions you may have an excellent candidate.

3. Deference: Self-confidence is fine, even necessary, in a salesperson. The best, however, attribute much of their success to luck, even as they work tirelessly to make it happen. They are humble, respectful, and grateful to their colleagues, clients, and mentors. They feel blessed to have had the opportunity to serve. They never bash their competition or their previous employer. Their background reflects a dedication to others, not just themselves. This characteristic of deference is as important as any other.

Deference may appear counter-intuitive. Shouldn't salespeople be a little cocky and money motivated? Not without some deference—if you want them to last. Those without deference may be able to sell, making an impact early in their tenure with a company, but that tenure often ends early with one of the following actions:

- The best start their own company and handle it with class.

- Many start their own company and immediately start poaching clients, because they believe they brought them in the first place.

- Some hop to another company with a higher base.

Adding fuel to the fire, sales leaders will overlook their behavior, because they're bringing in clients. This creates a disastrous long-term effect. You're basically sending the message to the rest of the organization that as long as you hit your numbers, you can play fast and loose with the rules. There are many excellent, aggressive sales reps that lack this third "D." They are driven, disciplined, and are on their third company in four years. When building a sales team for the long haul, your people must have some deference in their makeup.

Screening and Interviewing

Personality profiles, as a hiring tool, can be quite useful and are often excellent predictors of future behavior and work style. There is usually a cost per person for the test and the resulting analysis. There are many on the market, and you'll find common elements among the personality traits and motivators they reveal. It is not the intention of this chapter to catalogue and evaluate them—that would be a lengthy exercise—but from my experience of profiling and hiring hundreds of salespeople, there are two critical rules you should follow.

1. Look for drive. Most of these tools contain an element that rates the candidates tendency to persist through difficult situations, usually beginning with the letter D, "driver, dominant, director," and so forth. Almost without exception, you'll want your sales professional to have this trait in spades. Not only is it one of our essential "Ds," it is the key to overcoming rejection. Many believe that high sales performers don't take rejection personally. In reality, many do, but they drive through it because they are more motivated by goals other than by harmonious relationships with others. Candidates with dominant driver traits work fast, are not afraid to challenge their customers, often exceed their goals, and are blunt in their assessment of the marketplace. As their future manager, your primary challenge might be to keep them from upsetting others in the office, as the driver does not fear confrontation and the occasional debate. You may need to "dial them down" a bit, but this is a good problem to have.

2. Beware the overly analytical. Another common personality trait measured is the tendency toward numbers, tasks, and analytical thought. Look for the "thinker, problem-solver, detail-oriented" label. If this is an extremely dominant trait in your candidate, she would likely make an excellent accountant, actuary, or engineer, but don't hire her as a salesperson. Analytical personalities are often diligent and motivated

but they view client objections as problems to be solved. They often silently agree with them, and work to address them in a deliberate, step-by-step manner, believing their prospect will appreciate their hard work. All the while, a competitor will dig further into the real reason for the objection—which is usually not the stated reason the client gives, but one of perceived value—and make the sale. Moreover, if your position involves any type of networking or prospecting activity, trade show attendance and promotion, telephone prospecting, client mixers and events, and so forth, a dominant analytical will not enjoy that aspect of the job and it will drain their energy.

The Interview

The candidate interview can be unreliable if not conducted properly. Some of the best advice I have seen with regard to interviewing, especially as it applies to finding sales professionals, comes from this *Harvard Business Review* article, first published back in 1989:

> "Unlike your human resources people, you interview applicants only occasionally. You don't catch that duty often enough to hone your skills. The candidates themselves are likely to be more adroit than you… Recent experience on the job trail may have taught them all the right things to ask and say.
>
> Then there are the personal attributes that you bring to the interview. The aggressive characteristics that helped put you in an executive position also put obstacles in your way to becoming an expert interviewer—learning how to ask, to watch, and to listen. The take-charge attitude of many top executives makes it hard for them to keep their ears open and mouths shut—two critical characteristics of the expert interviewer."

In other words, when you're interviewing sales candidates, you may have to become someone you're not—a deliberate, detailed, and careful questioner and listener. Our fictional sales leaders, Blaire, Rob, and Curtis, probably prepared little for their interviews with Kirsten, Sonja, and Rory. But if you're to find candidates that possess the three Ds you're going to have to choose your questions carefully. And listen to the responses!

Use Behavioral-Based Interview Questions

Behavioral-based interviewing focuses on the idea that the best predictor of future performance is past performance in like circumstances. You should first prepare questions that probe for the essential traits and then prepare questions particular to the role. For example, if the selling cycle typically involves quick, high-pressure transactions, you might ask for an example of how the candidate has demonstrated an ability to juggle multiple prospects, prioritize them, and still manage to increase revenue. As you ask these questions, watch and listen closely, you'll find it's relatively easy to gauge the candidate's level of comfort and familiarity with the scenario you present to them. The following are lists of example questions for essential traits (drive, discipline, and deference), as well as other specific traits.

Drive:

- Tell me about a time when you landed an account where your prospect had a strong relationship with a competitor.

- Give me an example from your career when you set a difficult goal and achieved it beyond your expectations.

- Many times in this position, you may find yourself approaching strong prospects that seemingly have no interest in meeting with you. How have you overcome this in the past?

Discipline:

- Give me an example of when your goals were interrupted by circumstances beyond your control. How were you able to achieve them?

- Describe your approach when landing a big account. What process did you follow, and how did it contribute to your success?

- Tell me about a time when you were on the verge of losing an account, but were able to save it. How did you set about planning and achieving the goal of saving the business relationship?

Deference:

- How have you been able to positively influence your peers or team members to achieve a goal? Give a specific example.

- Give me an example of a significant personal or professional achievement where a little luck might have been involved.

- Who have been your mentors? Give me an example of where someone has had a positive influence on your career goals.

Selling cycle:

- Short: This role may require you to prioritize multiple prospects and land the most lucrative ones, sometimes within (time frame). Tell me about a time when you have done that successfully.

- Long: In this position, it may take as much as (time frame) to land a prospect or contract. Tell me about a time when you've done that successfully.

Handling adversity:

- Tell me about a time when you've lost an account through no fault of yours or your organization. How did you handle it?

- Tell me about a situation where market or economic conditions adversely affected your ability to make a sale. How did you respond?

Self-motivation:

- Describe for me a typical day. How do you set out to achieve your goals on a day-to-day basis?

- This role will often require you to work with minimal supervision. Give me an example of a time when you've worked in such an environment successfully.

Working in a large, matrixed organization:

- In our company, you may have several key stakeholders to satisfy. Give me an example where you successfully satisfied the needs of stakeholders at multiple levels.

- Give me an example of when you may have unknowingly upset someone in your organization. How did you handle it?

Hunting versus gathering:

- This position will require you to bring in new business from both new and existing accounts. From your previous roles, how have you done that?

- Tell me about a time when you had to land new business from an account that had never heard of your company. How were you able to win them over?

Candidate Answers: Look for the Difference Makers

With this strategy, it is difficult for a candidate to charm their way through the interview because rather than looking for good answers, you're looking for good sales behavior patterns in the candidate's experience, what we call the three difference makers.

- **Applicable experience:** The right salesperson for your organization may not have a rehearsed, pitch-perfect answer, but they will readily draw upon their experience to address the question.

- **Clarifying questioning skill:** Look for the candidate that asks good clarifying questions showing an excellent indicator of solid sales ability.

- **Storytelling acumen:** Does the candidate possess the ability to express themselves in a cohesive, thoughtful example? Look for the candidate that tells a compelling story displaying another effective trait in the successful sales professional.

Summing It Up

Let's take a moment to revisit our three fictional sales leaders.

Blaire decided to have a heart-to-heart with Kirsten. Together they decided that the role she was in, which required patience with a lengthy, complex selling process, wasn't right for her. Kirsten understood and moved on, while Blaire decided to prepare a list that focused on her essential specific traits to fill that role: patience with the selling cycle, persistence in the face of adversity, and a belief in their company's solution.

Rob realized that maybe his intuition wasn't the best method to find his next candidate. Upon reflection, he recognized that over the years, he had more misses than hits. Partnering with his human resources director, they developed the ideal profile for an assistant director of sales at his hotel, chose a profiling tool, and started anew. Sonja, ever popular, was recruited by the catering department, and is now happily planning weddings and events.

Curtis turned the hiring process over to Brenda after Rory chose to go back to school. Brenda, understanding that Curtis was a great salesperson but a disastrous manager, took over the day-to-day management of the office and set about finding Curtis' future successor, someone who could work with minimal supervision and had the drive and discipline to prospect from Curtis' massive list of leads.

What's Next

What will you do? As you approach your next prospective sales candidate, you must accept one fundamental truth that escapes even the most thoughtful and reflective sales leaders.

It is not easy to find sales talent. It never has been. These tactics and strategies will help you. They are meant to apply some science and method to the messy world of evaluating human potential. As we've pointed out, hiring salespeople is more art than science, and often brings more trial and tribulation than comfort. Rather than dread it, expect it. The rewards are great for building a solid team of sales professionals, or even for finding one high performer.

Action Plan

For your next round of interviews:

- Research personality profiling tools, and select one that fits your budget and needs.

- Prepare a list of questions to identify the essential traits: drive, discipline, and deference.
- Consider the specific traits required by the sales position for which you are hiring. From your list, choose the most crucial to success.
- Develop questions for your desired specific traits.

In your next interviews, listen and watch for the three difference makers: ready experience, questioning, and storytelling.

Review the myths: Do any of these apply to you? If so, develop a plan to remind yourself to watch for them in the future.

References

Collins, J. (2001). *Good to Great*. New York: Harper Collins.

About the Author

Joseph Anzalone, the director of the school of sales for Hilton Worldwide, is a sales and training executive with a 15-year track record of designing and delivering sales training programs. Prior to joining Hilton Worldwide, Joe was VP of sales and training for Asset Marketing Systems (AMS), a financial services and insurance marketing organization. While at AMS, Joe built a training organization that delivered sales learning to more than 3,000 independent advisors across the United States. Prior to his career in training, Joe was an outside sales representative, and has experience telemarketing, cold calling, and working on a sales quota requirement and a straight commission compensation plan.

10
Strategic Storytelling for Sales Managers

Alfredo Castro

As organizations become more geographically distributed and competition increases, the communication challenges that a global salesforce faces also increase. Sales managers need to find new ways communicate with their salesforce and their customers; storytelling is a very powerful way to do this. If used properly, it will differentiate your products and services from the rest.

Storytelling for Business?

During the weekly virtual team meeting, David, one of John's sales team members, was explaining how difficult it would be to set up a meeting with one of the prospective customers in his region: "She does not like long explanations or technical presentations. I can't make a sale using our sales approach!"

John, a successful regional sales manager, said: "I understand what you're saying. Use stories to engage this customer."

A surprised David replied: "Stories? Those were great when we were kids! How are they going to help with my sales calls?"

John would have to explain how stories can be powerful and strategic tools in a business environment.

Why should a sales manager be interested in storytelling?

CEOs and entrepreneurs are beginning to recognize that a virtual salesforce not only cuts down on costs, but can also add a competitive advantage. By the end of the decade, nearly a billion people across the globe will be mobile workers! One of the key things this new virtual approach brings to the table is the use of storytelling. Mobile workers tend to use social media to keep in touch. Guess what? Social media is really a technical version of storytelling. The use of social media is still in the beginning stages and increased use will stimulate the use of more stories.

Understanding Business Storytelling

Stories create a communication bridge to connect the left and right sides of the brain, by touching the rational elements of our customers (and team members) as well as their emotional aims and objectives. Storytelling in the corporate environment is generally used in marketing and product development. This technique can also be used in other areas to improve results. One of the best places to use storytelling is sales management. One of most powerful ways to engage a sales team and the customers is to use storytelling. Although it's a natural competence for many salespeople, not all sales managers are able to tell effective stories to their sales team or customers.

Stories are useful conduits for reinforcing your business priorities and values, because they will help sales representatives to better understand what corporate values mean in terms of behavior.

For example, it is one thing to say that the organization values integrity. But to tell a story of how integrity saved $1 billion during a situation with a sales customer, is another thing all together.

Like any good story, we'll start at the beginning. To make it simple, here's my definition of strategic storytelling for sales management: Storytelling is the art of telling a story that will engage listeners, by providing a link between facts and emotions. The storyline must make sense during the beginning, middle, and end, with actions made by a memorable character. That character must achieve a goal through a sequence of events that engage the listeners and create emotional experiences for them, so that they can experience the story again and again to feel the same emotions as the first time the story was told!

It is easy and natural. If you are wondering, "What is in it for me?" try to remember three real situations you have faced in your day-to-day sales management that fit this definition. As sales managers, we should be able to tell and remember many stories that express our routine and our challenges.

By telling stories we can explain to the sales professionals who report to us how to approach a customer, how to apply the sales methodology learned in the corporate university, and how to be successful in this beautiful science of selling.

Storytelling is something well recognized by professionals from a variety of disciplines such as historians, literary critics, filmmakers, cognitive psychologists, lawyers, neurologists, physicians, economists, and, yes, professional storytellers. As F. Scott Fitzgerald said: "Draw your chair up to edge of the precipice, and I'll tell you a story."

Sales Management Using Strategic Storytelling

As a sales manager, how and where do we start looking for stories? To make it simple and applicable, the majority of our stories regarding the sales processes will come from events or relationships.

Examining the events we attend during our sales routines we can recognize many small stories that relate how we can act, react, and interact with our team and customers.

Relationships are also a good source for stories. The tense we use is an important element in crafting a story. For example, some events from past experiences, when properly understood and told, will lead you to future events. One of the most important reasons for crafting a good story from a past experience is to make conclusions to improve the impact of the events you will be organizing in the future. In some stories, relationships and their outcomes can be the main purpose of what is being told, while in other stories, the relationships will be a peripheral element to the story.

Learning from scientists, we know that our intuition is very important for creating, telling, and understanding stories. Once we can understand the main elements of a narrative, intuitively we make connections with our day-to-day imagining the scenes, emotions, and characters. For example, at the very beginning of this chapter I told you one portion of a story that really happened between David and John. As you read each line, your brain probably started to imagine how John would react by listening David's comments.

There are no rigid formulas to determine how long a story should be. Starting with the message is a key difference between strategic storytelling and the informal storytelling that occurs every day in organizations. In strategic storytelling, the message comes first, and you identify and develop stories around it. You can use storytelling as part of a formal communication plan in which you give careful consideration to the key messages sales professionals need to understand and use to guide their daily work. However, in a business environment, we have to consider these elements:

- What purpose do you want to achieve with that story?
- Who is involved (the characters)?
- What's the time frame (past, present, or future)?
- Who should tell the story?

You should also consider what I call my three golden rules for sales management.

Golden Rules:

1. The story is based on a lesson learned.

2. The story can be used in a sales-business context.

3. The story must search for better performance.

The Story Is Based on a Lesson Learned

As a manager, you know that your sales professionals will learn from procedures and policies if they are translated to a lesson that can be learned. People use lists all the time, but can't always remember what's on that list. Only a narrative can integrate the listed items into a logical process, enabling the person to remember how to approach a situation (and how to react to that scenario). Behaviors can be improved and repeated if they are told in a logical sequence that makes sense and is memorable. This is what I mean by lesson learned.

The Story Can Be Used in a Sales Business Context

The main purpose for using storytelling is to enable your staff to use the right behaviors in a business situation. In order to create a credible, realistic, and tangible impact, sales managers should use the storytelling elements properly to focus the story on specific actions to achieve success. This will provide engagement, emotion, logic, and authenticity in the manager's communications with the sales staff. The story must make a point about sales, customer service, business improvement, innovation, leadership, communication, teamwork, productivity, or other topics related to the workplace.

The Story Must Search for Better Performance

How many stories can a sales professional tell? Professionals in other areas used to call salespeople storytellers. But, you must be careful: The best stories are those that are based on real-life moments. The manager must be able to remember the sequence of events and the relationships in colorful detail. Doug Stevenson, author of *Theatre Business Stories* explains it this way: "I call these events 'Polaroid memories,' because you can clearly see them in your mind's eye. When you recall the event or relationship; the time, place, and specific details such as how it sounded, looked, and felt come back easily and vividly."

A good story in a business context doesn't just have to be true; it must call for an improvement in performance. We all know that the business environment and the market are full of challenges, competition, and obstacles. Our staff is counting on us to deliver a redeeming message that will make them remember what do to and say when they are in front of their customers in a challenging situation. They need us to remind them that the sale can be made, even with the barriers, objections, and tactics used by our customers. A story (and not only a list of steps to be taken) will enable them to enhance performance and achieve positive outcomes because it provides ways of remembering actions to overcome a difficult situation.

In a sales environment, another advantage of using storytelling is using stories as metaphors. When facing a difficult situation a manager can make use of a metaphor so that the difficult issue can be more easily understood by the sales professional. For example, think about stories we knew in our childhood: the majority used metaphors to communicate the appropriate action to be taken.

Leaders and Storytelling

In many languages spoken all over the world there will be a similarity between these words: leader and manager. In English sometimes we use them synonymously, but let's understand the real meaning behind each. The manager is the professional who is in charge of executing the management of a business unit and its team of professionals. A leader is the person who uses their experience and insight to coach and lead others to solve problems. I like to say in my workshops: The real truth is that every leader may not be a manager, but every manager should be a leader.

Management and leadership aren't the same thing, but can be combined in one person if he or she knows how to use the formal responsibilities to create an opportunity to take on the informal responsibilities of leadership. This change process does not happen easily, and that is why companies invest in developing their new sale managers to help them become the leader of their team.

Storytelling can help this transition move more quickly. Sales leaders should focus on stories that will:

- stimulate a learning workplace
- credit their team
- recognize and reward improvement.

Here are some tips to help you move from a sales manager to a sales leader.

Sales Leaders Tell Stories to Stimulate a Learning Workplace

Stories can be a very powerful way to create a learning organization environment where sales staff search for solutions to mitigate problems, and avoid errors and mistakes. Beware of sales managers who are not leaders. They tend to criticize mistakes and perpetuate an organizational climate that will be known for fear and blame. They tell stories to explain mistakes and point out who made them. This is not a positive use of storytelling and creates a barrier to risk taking and learning.

To be a sales leader who uses storytelling to build up your environment, be careful about the purpose of the stories you tell. For example, pointing out your sales staff's mistakes directly may be assertive, but this may also leave them feeling embarrassed and frustrated. Tell stories about the issue, not about the person. Being a learning organization is an excellent way to generate good results. Another good example is making a statistical analysis on types of mistakes, and creating stories where they can remember procedures to avoid those mistakes. Good sales leaders give their team the chance to learn and grow through real problems and solutions told in stories.

Sales Leaders Tell Stories to Credit Their Team

Managers tell stories because they want credit for good results. It is interesting how they, apparently, seem to be working alone, without involving the team in the positive actions that generated the good results. Sales leaders credit their teams for achieving good results, and tell stories to the high-level management about how their team deals with challenges. Effective leaders also share stories that credit their teams for the big wins and create an environment where new sales professionals join the team and learn from seasoned colleagues to drive success as a team. This will pay off in the long run by creating a workplace with a collaborative culture.

Sales Leaders Tell Stories of Hope to Recognize and Reward Improvement

Many managers forget to praise their subordinates. Leaders reward even the smallest improvement. Praise pays off when it comes to increasing the overall success of your team or company. As a sales leader, create stories and make time to recognize your staff for even the smallest accomplishment. It will only increase their interest in what they do. If you're interested in ensuring your staff takes pride in all that they do, regularly give coaching and feedback, always mentioning their improvement. Creating moments of recognition by sharing good example stories can help other sales professionals remember and repeat success. Everyone wants to be genuinely appreciated for their efforts, and recognized for their improvement.

A sales leader tells stories of hope, while a manager who is not a leader focuses only on poor performance by telling stories of fear. This comes down to that well-known metaphor: seeing the cup half empty or half full.

Managing Gen Y Sales Professionals With Storytelling

"If you want happiness for a lifetime—help the next generation."

—*Chinese Proverb*

I found this proverb in a historical temple 30 km out of Beijing, China. This illustrates what has been said about managing Generation Y. We have had generational conflicts since society started to draw pictures on stone walls centuries ago! The only difference now is that the Baby Boomers and Gen Xers are among three to four generations in the sales workplace.

Depending on the country, company, and segment, Gen Y employees may account for more than 35 percent of the sales workforce. Like any group of people, you will find some difficult or impossible to manage, but with most, you'll do just fine as long as you're willing to work with their idiosyncrasies.

For example, take the story of Beth, a Millennial who has worked for a manufacturing company for two years. She was recently promoted to sales administration supervisor. Last time we met she told me: "I never wake up dreading to go to work. As cliché as it sounds, we are like one crazy family. This is a fun place to work, everyone is relaxed, and customers love us. I am constantly being challenged with new things to do in addition to the items already on my to-do list. I have two bosses and I get feedback, mostly positive, from one of them at least once a day. If they say something critical, they do it in a nice way and this is a part of my job that I like so much. I trust and respect my bosses, and I know I can count on them in tough situations. They're there for me when I need them and I can tell they care about me. If it weren't for them, I don't think I would like this job nearly as much as I do." You would like to be Beth's sales manager, wouldn't you?

We don't always hear this because we may be adopting a leadership style that does not engage our Gen Y sales professionals. My advice for managing Generation Y is to use storytelling to lead them and create an environment of engagement and motivation.

As a sales manager, we have to understand that the generation coming into the workplace now was raised using online collaboration tools to build large online networks, which means that they were in a world of stories and connection. The relationship with their online community is something that people who have not worked in this way won't understand. The comment you hear from someone who doesn't participate in the social tech world is: "These young people just sit around texting and playing on Facebook all day." Does this sound familiar? We have to recognize that this generation is nurturing a network that they leverage in powerful ways to get their jobs done and live their lives, and this is the future way of doing business in sales.

Maybe just blocking social technology usage is simpler, but, to be honest, this is a poor option because organizations need social tools to communicate with customers, management, vendors, and partners. The dynamics of how the next generation will operate, and how many older people must adapt, deserve an immense amount of attention because it's a new way to get things done. Managing people in an electronic sales environment will be the main challenge for sales managers in the next decade.

Another issue in a world of social media is the viral effects of the shared social comments. Once someone clicks the send button, words, pictures, videos, or presentations are out of our control. This information is easily searchable and can be read by virtually anyone on the web. This can have serious repercussions for organizations as more people begin to use their own discretion in what they say about the organization publicly.

Sales managers need to step into the breach and help employees understand what is appropriate to discuss online when talking about the organization or while posting using their employee job title. I am already seeing many painful stories of people who, without thinking, posted information or content that came back to haunt both them and the organization. Let's look at some real stories of mistakes people have made:

A sales representative of a multinational electronic company posts what he thinks is a funny video of his sales manager singing at a company party. The video goes viral and is ridiculed as an amateur act by leadership.

A new salesperson attending a meeting at a publicly traded company hears a comment about sales being off by a large percentage this quarter and repeats the conversation to friends on Facebook. The press picks up this post on an alert they run on the company and goes public with a comment that was meant to be internal. This leads to embarrassment for the company when the story goes public in the mainstream press.

In order to improve your ability to manage a Generation Y team and avoid potential social media problems, I suggest these tips:

- Implement a culture of storytelling that shares stories of success.

- Share more information with your sales professionals about the business, customer complaints, profitability, and related matters, using multimedia processes.

- Help team members work together within new boundaries, creating a risk-taking culture, and valuing experiences from both older and younger members.

- Resist the temptation to slide back into the comfort of your old role (the way you were managed in the past), especially during crisis situations or technically complex problems in different sales steps.

- Recognize attitudes and behaviors of members to build a culture of collective team learning approach—independent from their time working in sales.

Using Storytelling on Virtual Sales Teams

In a virtual environment it's really difficult to read how the other person is receiving the message, or to even know what to say next. How can a manager lead a virtual sales team? They can use storytelling!

On some level, virtual salespeople have existed since the telephone was invented, when road warriors would call in sales figures at the end of the week. But those relationships between salesperson and manager were often rooted in deep personal connections developed during time spent in the office. Like any great sales team, virtual or not, you'll want to be sure that you're finding the right path to lead this sales professional. The problem is how to engage them. The challenges of virtual workers are not limited to geography. It may include the concept of "virtual distance," which is the idea that the technology people use to connect can actually drive people apart.

To achieve real results from a salesforce, a manager must relate to them on a human level, working on building a relationship that can be trusted. This can be done using storytelling. For example, sales managers should be willing to offer information about their personal lives, and be receptive to listening to the issues their employees are concerned about. Building this trust can be even more important for a virtual salesperson. Let me put it this way: It is not the principles of leading that are different. It's the practices that make the difference.

If you're leading a virtual team, you'll need to set the tone for not only how sales professionals interact with potential customers, but also with each other. From the very beginning identify the boundaries, and enforce them constantly. Sales professionals should understand how and when to get in touch, and how often they're expected to check in. In a weekly virtual meeting, tell stories and ask for them—it's about creating a high-touch environment. It's immediate and real time.

Consider these seven tips:

1. Acknowledge the challenges of virtual working to the team. Tell stories of how you want to lead them, and how you want them sharing their professional experiences.

2. Use storytelling principles while integrating mobile practices and technology into existing formal sales systems.

3. Keep policies straightforward and technology simple to use.

4. Define roles and expectations using examples and good stories.

5. Use happy-ending stories to create a culture of success, but also tell bad-ending stories to explain what should be avoided on the sales field, when the sales manager is not there with them physically.

6. Using storytelling platforms, invest in sharing, training, learning, and improvement.

7. Support mobile workers as if they were customers.

Don't forget that it's up to the sales leader to motivate his or her sales team! In a virtual setting, sales professionals will lack the face-to-face feedback that's often built into office culture. Virtual employees can often feel that nothing they do matters; after all, it's hard to see tangible results far from the nucleus of the company.

Summing It Up

This chapter proposes the practical use of business storytelling for sales managers. It is never too late to start storytelling!

I urge you to apply the tips, principles, and recommendations to see the impact you will have on the business results. More than that, you will create a culture of engagement and better equip your sales professionals.

Learning how to craft and tell stories in a systematic way will make the difference. Here's what well-known writer, Steven Denning, wrote: "Leadership is about change, about new ways of working. Successful leaders are the ones who can draw up stories to help people understand what they are facing and motivate them to move toward the future."

Whatever you do, don't stop! In order to improve your knowledge, search for books, workshops, webinars, and articles that will help you tell better stories. Practice your storytelling skills every day. Last but not least, would you like to know what happened with the two characters from the very beginning of this chapter?

A Successful Story

Two weeks later, after learning from his manager how storytelling can be useful in a business environment, David called John to say: "I have never thought that using stories would help me so much. I set up the meeting with the customer for tomorrow! Can you imagine how engaging it was using a good story with her?"

A proud John replied: "Congratulations, David! Can you tell me how you did it? Tell me the story..."

Action Plan

It is time for a happy ending! In order to use storytelling as a sales manager and obtain good results from it, review the tips carefully and think about how to apply them to your situation. The more you apply stories in a sales environment, the more comfortable you will feel and the easier it will be to identify the impact it generates. Once you decide to use stories more strategically in your sales organization, a natural question will be where to begin. As a proposed action plan, try these three practical activities in your day-to-day work life.

Worksheet: Craft a Story

Prepare a three-minute story in a sales environment, to be told in the next meeting with your sales team. Use this template:

Table 10.1

Storytelling Element	Guiding Questions	Your Story
Understand the context (Preparation)	Think about the sales context: What is the key point I want to make? What is the central situation or event I plan to describe? What is the point of view of the main character(s) in this story?	
Introduction (Beginning)	What, specifically, will I say to begin this story? What will I say to introduce the character(s) and the setting of this story?	
Challenge (Extraordinary goal or objective to be overcome)	How will I describe the problem or issue faced by my character(s)?	
Actions	What actions does he/she take to resolve this problem?	
Impacts	What happens as a result of these actions?	
Moral	What is the underlying meaning or frame for this story?	

Team-Building Activity: Craft a Story

During my time as actor, I learned a technique that in a world of theatre we call the backstory. An actor creates a backstory to help explain the character's motivation. The actor may or may not share this backstory with others, but it is important that the actor knows why the character behaves in specific ways, says specific words, and takes specific actions. When the backstory is effective, the character created by the actor seems believable to an audience. When team members share their backstory there is an opportunity for deeper awareness and collaboration.

Process:

1. Have the team form a circle, sitting or standing.

2. Pose the question: "What in your past, considering the sales environment experience, has shaped who you are today?"

3. Present your backstory by disclosing a specific incident in your past that has shaped your character or skills. Be authentic, open, and sincere.

4. Invite the next person to speak by asking: "What in your past has shaped who you are today as a salesperson?"

5. After each backstory, thank the participant for sharing it.

6. After all backstories have been shared, acknowledge the team for their willingness to share

Debrief: Ask the following questions: How do you feel now that you've learned more about the people on your team? What did you learn today that would help you be a more effective team member?

Remembering Your Audience: Craft a Story to Impact a Presentation or a Speech

Storytelling is an effective leadership communication tool because it is so natural and simple. It is also very powerful in a customer presentation, in difficult meetings, or during proposal presentations. You may find it useful to think upfront about your messages and your stories, experimenting with the tools and practicing your delivery. When you start telling your stories, consider the impact on your audience. With time and practice, this technique will become second nature, and the steps, and your stories, will flow seamlessly.

1. When implementing a storytelling framework in a presentation situation, it is good to focus on a few key messages. A good question to ask is, "What are the three key messages I want my audience to remember?"

2. Work to identify, develop, and share stories that reinforce those messages. This helps you build an integrated and consistent communication strategy and enables you to personalize the message in an intimate and authentic way at the same time. Be careful and try to avoid "Pay attention because I will tell you a short story." Instead, try to start by saying "for example," "the other day," or "you will not believe what I felt at that meeting. Let me tell you."

3. Create a structure for your story using storytelling principles (beginning, middle, end, logic comes with emotions, and an extraordinary character trying to solve an extraordinary challenge), and the three basic elements of a business story: context, action, and impact.

Context sets the scene for the situation: previous meetings, agreements with the customer, and problems or solutions implemented, along with the relationship with the customer.

Action moves us from the beginning to the impact. The story has a beginning, middle, and an end. As defined by Aristotle, to be considered a beginning, this portion of story requires nothing to precede it. An end is what requires nothing to follow it. The middle of story needs something both before and after it.

Impact is the outcome of that narrative. For the storyteller, this means the need to choose the starting and end point in order to produce the moral or example of the story.

References

Stevenson, D. (2008). *Story Theater Method.* Colorado Springs, CO: Cornelia Press.

Denning, S. (2010). *The Leader's Guide to Radical Management.* San Francisco: Jossey-Bass.

About the Author

Alfredo Castro is the president of MOT Training and Development, Inc. a consulting company based in Miami; Sao Paulo, Brazil; and Lisbon, Portugal. Alfredo was the chairman of the ASTD Advisory Board 2010 (ICE Chicago) based in Washington, D.C. He is the director of the Brazilian T&D Association and author of nine business books. His international business consultant experience is in implementing blended learning programs and human resource projects in more than 120 companies, and more than 25 countries in Asia, Africa, Europe, and the Americas.

11
Social Media Marketing for Sales Managers

Glenn Raines

The emergence of social media and social media networking in recent years is presenting sales managers with unprecedented opportunities to lower the cost of new customer acquisitions, retention, and loyalty. Furthermore, the technical functions behind social media marketing allows peers to share relevant and valuable content so your company benefits from being referred within already established trust relationships. This chapter will provide an overview of some of the basic principles, tactics, and technology platforms you can use immediately to effectively manage a social media marketing effort within your own sales organization. In turn, some of the points addressed will provide you the knowledge to work with your marketing department to effectively promote and engage your target customers.

Social Thought Leadership, Attraction Marketing, and the New Sales Conversion Funnel

The effective use of social media in promoting products and services is turning push marketing on its head. Today, it's all about attraction marketing: the idea of engaging in social media communities where your sales team members can establish themselves as the go-to person to solve a problem or provide useful information to a customer prospect. This is the new "pure gold" in customer prospecting because now your sales team member can directly engage the potential buyer who has expressed that they are actively seeking resolution to their problem. Your sales team member has their attention. By positioning them as credible subject matter experts within social media networking communities, you are, in essence, creating effective brand ambassadors who are in the right place at the right time to answer the right question for a customer prospect. This dynamic exchange can lead to developing warm relationships, earning trust, and leading the customer prospect toward sales conversion. It's important to note that social media and the Internet in general have made the sales conversion funnel more complex than ever before. It used to be that customer prospects had few options to get information to make a purchasing decision. Typically the prospect relied on the company's own sales materials or customer testimonials. But today, customer prospects have the power of the mouse to search for independent, objective third-party reviews about the performance quality of a company's products or services. In turn, search results from Google serve up an avalanche of information on the web for one to explore and make more informed purchasing decisions.

This creates a situation of a multitude of touchpoints that can influence a customer prospect's purchasing decision. These touch points include results from Internet searches, exploring branded Facebook and Twitter pages, checking sales team member LinkedIn profiles, and even asking their trusted peers and friends for their recommendations. As a sales manager, you have an opportunity to align your branded content with the subject matter expertise of your team members, satisfied customers, and other activities within this more complex sales conversion funnel. In doing so, you're creating the opportunity to be in the right place at the right time to engage the customer prospect when they are looking for an answer and when they are in the market to buy.

Aligning with Brand Marketing to Execute an Effective Social Media Selling Effort

When social media first came on the scene it was primarily the responsibility of the marketing department. That still holds true today. However, social media, as a corporate function, is finding its way into other departments of the company such as customer service and investor relations. As social media matures as a business process, company departments outside marketing are establishing best practices that embrace social media to drive their own initiatives in synergistic ways that work in parallel with the marketing department's social media strategy and tactics. The balance of this chapter outlines tactics and tools you, as a sales management leader, can execute within your sales department that can work in harmony with marketing, while achieving your goals of getting your sales team out in social media communities to identify, pre-qualify, engage, and offer value to customer prospects leading to sales conversion and measureable results.

A Sustainable Social Media Selling Effort Must Align With Company-Wide Business Goals

Executing an effective, manageable, and sustainable social media selling strategy must take into account the importance of aligning your social selling strategy with the overall company business plan and brand marketing communications strategy already baked into the annual marketing plan. It's highly recommended to meet with your marketing team and learn their plans for social media brand strategy. This is also an ideal time to express your interest to the marketing department in leveraging social media with your sales team to identify, engage, and acquire new customers. At this point, the marketing team may have some ideas on messaging and content your team can use and distribute through their individual LinkedIn profiles. More ideas on these tactics are detailed later in this chapter. Once you know the social media strategy plans of your marketing department, you'll want to plan and execute your social media selling tactics in the right sequence. For example, you'll want to have sales team member LinkedIn profiles upgraded first before engaging customer prospects, because prospects will research the LinkedIn profile of your sales team member to assess whether to take the conversation to the next level. To borrow a metaphor, imagine you're a new home builder that needs to attract prospective home buyers. First, you construct the main foundation and frame. Next, you add the basic features all new homeowners need. Once completed, you're confident to hold an open house to attract prospective buyers. At this stage, you become a careful listener to learn what the unmet needs of the new home buyer are and what amenities they want in a new home. You then take this insight and show the prospective home buyer the amenities you can add to meet their specific needs.

Social Selling Tip

In social selling, effective engagement with customer prospects first acknowledges their problem, then demonstrates relevant solutions through storytelling of case studies.

This gives the product contextual value that solved a problem or achieved the desired outcome. A distinct advantage that social selling offers is the insight you gain in social conversations with your customer prospects and current customers. Even criticism and negative sentiment around your products can provide valuable insight that can help you continuously improve your products and services. The balance of this chapter will outline the tactics you can sequentially execute to establish, manage, and sustain a social media selling strategy.

Table 11.1: The Importance of Sequencing a Social Media Selling Tactical Execution

Phases	Tactics	Examples
Phase 1: Align social media strategy with key business objectives.	• Identify primary business objectives.	• Become the "trusted industry leader."
	• Align social selling with business, marketing, and sales objectives.	• How will marketing and sales support?
	• Leverage brand messaging for creative execution.	• How can paid advertising drive social engagement?
	• Align social media tactics with all objectives.	• How will social media help achieve sales goals like new customer acquisition and retention benchmarks?
Phase 2: Establish a social media foundation.	• Identify branded content for social media repurposing.	• Compliance-approved whitepapers, PowerPoint presentations.
	• Assess subject matter expertise of sales team members.	• Niche specialty, customer testimonials, authorships.
	• Implement social media profiles.	• LinkedIn, Google+ profiles.
	• Implement social media customer touchpoints.	• Social media links one mail signatures, business cards, stickers.
	• Identify key social media metrics for success.	• Increase customer inquiries, RFPs, sales activity spikes.

	• Deploy a social media listening strategy.	• Tools: Social Mention, Google Alerts.
Phase 3: Understand the customers needs.	• Understand the "what, where, and who."	• Unmet customer needs, where customer prospects are already talking, who is talking, and their potential influence.
	• Evolve social media sales content strategy.	• Leverage LinkedIn activity updates.
Phase 4: Engage customers based on valued relevance.	• Build a quality social media network.	• LinkedIn Advanced Search, connect, warm referrals.
	• Be the big fish in a small pond.	• Convey subject matter expertise in niche LinkedIn groups.

Align Social Media Strategy With Key Business Objectives

The sales conversion path within this more complex funnel begins with a strategic planning approach that recognizes social media marketing tactics must be executed in the right sequence and accurately aligned with key business and brand communications objectives that are already part of the annual planning of your company.

The first step in mapping out a social media strategy for your sales team is to ensure that your strategic and tactical activities on social media are tightly aligned with the business objectives and the marketing communications executed by your brand marketing team and the advertising agency (if in play). This right alignment will ensure that you and your sales team are executing a social selling effort that delivers on your company's brand promise. By aligning your social selling strategy with the business objectives and brand marketing execution, you'll have a much clearer road map to what you should be doing with your tactical execution. For example, you might identify opportunities to make your sales materials more accessible through the LinkedIn profiles of your sales team or through links on a branded Twitter feed. While you may be limited in executing some efforts of social media through your sales department, it's worth the effort to work with your marketing team to see how best you can support the brand through your social selling customer engagement efforts. The reality is to manage what you can.

The key takeaway is to present your sales message and opportunity to close a sale at the most receptive point of customer engagement across social channels.

Figure 11.1

The Cold Call Is Dead: Introducing the New Lead Generation Opportunties

Effective selling in today's social media environment is more about attraction marketing versus push marketing. As a sales manager, you have the opportunity to leverage key social media platforms, tools, and industry-niched social communities as part of your lead generation program. Lead generation, in this new world, can involve three primary functions of social media tools.

- Social listening: Determine who is talking, what are they talking about, and where are they talking. This is the first step in generating new leads based on learning about the unment needs and challenges of customer prospects and how your company can offer a solution.

- Advanced search: Social media is not about generating leads on companies, but rather, building relationships with people affiliated with your target companies. LinkedIn, for example, has a robust advanced search function that allows you to find people at target companies so you can reach out to them if you belong to the same LinkedIn group, or get introduced through a mutual business colleague who is already connected to that person at the first degree network level.

- Push alerts: Emerging social media tools let you set up alerts that come into your email inbox notifying you of activities that happen at your target customer companies such as key personnel changes, new product or service introductions, and other changes that may present an opportunity for you to engage your company's services. Tools like Google Alerts and Social Mention let you set up alerts so you can engage customer prospects at the right time of need.

Again, strategic sequencing of your social media selling efforts is key:

- Know what marketing is doing in social media and leverage those opportunities.

- Establish a solid social media digital footprint for your sales team. LinkedIn profiles are the easiest and most widely viewed in the business community.

- Take pre-approved content and messaging you learned from marketing and repurpose it through LinkedIn profiles.

- Activate a lead generation program.

- Engage with customer prospect by offering value first—non-branded tips to show you care about them, and not about making the sale first.

The point is to make you and your sales team relevant and valued by customer prospects as subject matter experts who share knowledge and solutions that can lead to building trust relationships and eventually, sales opportunities.

The diagram on the following page illustrates how you can execute a plan to move your sales team out into the key social media platforms and social communities, activate engagement plans, and schedule a content strategy that provides information and links to drive traffic back to your company's branded websites and social media properties.

This strategy, if planned well, can make your social media initiatives from the sales department not only work politically well within your company, but also make your colleagues in marketing look good by your social selling and engagement tactics that drive more customer prospects to your company's branded social media and websites.

Figure 11.2

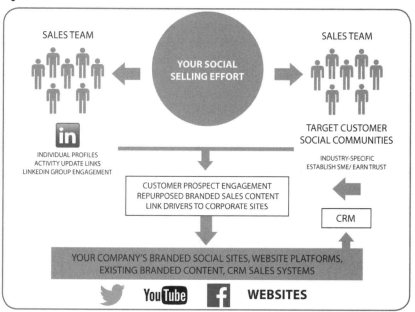

As this diagram illustrates, you can execute an effective social selling effort that is manageable within your area of sales management responsibility. The process focuses on three primary tactical initiatives:

- Deploy your sales team members out to social networks where your customer prospects are already having conversations, and are motivated to buy because they are asking questions. You and your sales team can proactively add value in these conversations that are already halfway to a sales close!

- Direct your sales team to earn customer trust first by answering questions, offering tips, and sharing knowledge that is "non-branded" and doesn't blantantly push your products and services. Here, the old adage applies, "People don't like to be sold—but they do like to buy!" Once trust is earned, the customer prospects will be more receptive to listen to how your products or services could be a solution.

- Repurpose branded sales collateral and make it more accessible on social sites for customer prospects with a content strategy that includes links to download materials, or directs them to more detailed information on your company's website.

- Devise a sales content strategy that drives customer engagement and website traffic to your company's branded online properties: social media sites, and websites, ultimately leading to prospect CRM to commence the sales conversion process.

You can leverage LinkedIn by enhancing the individual profiles of your sales team members: adding links to branded sales content using the LinkedIn activity update feature, adding rich media links to drive traffic, and having your team members assigned to engage in specific LinkedIn groups where target customer prospects gather, share information, or look for business solutions. Likewise, there are other industry-niched social communities beyond LinkedIn where your sales team can infiltrate, share their knowledge and content, and build their subject matter expertise to earn the trust of target customer prospects. This could be a win-win across the company, while avoiding the internal politics of who "owns" the social media effort for your company. Your goal is to leverage social media in your world to engage customers and drive sales results.

Establish a Social Media Foundation

There are three key initiatives you can execute to quickly establish a foundation for your social selling efforts:

1. Leverage existing branded content and sales materials that can be accessed on social media.

2. Build out more robust social media profiles for your individual sales team members on LinkedIn.

3. Position your sales team members as the go-to subject matter experts in niche social media communities.

First and foremost is the opportunity to get a greater return from your investment in existing sales materials. Social media networking platforms like LinkedIn provide functions to distribute your sales material and content through the individual LinkedIn profiles of your sales team members. Furthermore, by leveraging existing branded sales materials, you ensure that your social selling and engagement activities are aligned with the social media brand marketing efforts being driven by your marketing colleagues.

As the following diagram outlines, another key benefit of distributing existing branded sales content through the profiles of your sales team members is the opportunity to exponentially increase the exposure of your branded sales message across the separate social networks of each team member. For example, if your sales team of 10 members has, on average, 500 people in their respective LinkedIn network, your sales information can potentially reach over 5,000 people. This is a highly efficient and cost effective way to build awareness.

Figure 11.3

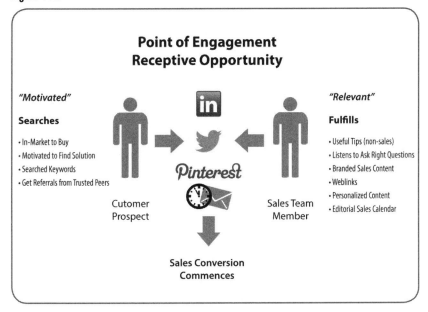

Collaborate closely with your brand marketing colleagues to see how they can help you:

- Assess what sales materials can be leveraged for distribution on social networking sites such as LinkedIn.
- Create an editorial calendar that schedules distribution of your sales content aligned with your company's branded marketing and sales promotional campaigns already in your company's annual marketing plan.

Select the right rich media links to use in your sales teams' LinkedIn profiles that display branded content links back to your company's website and other branded properties like online product information and other pages.

The Sales Team Member Social Graph—Engaging Customer Prospects at Key Touchpoints of Engagement

A social graph is simply a mapping plan to connect all the touchpoints where you and your sales team members may engage a highly receptive customer prospect. This is a golden opportunity to be relevant and valued by sharing knowledge and offering useful tips, which are actions that can lead to sales conversion. The following is a high-level view of a social graph illustrating the social platforms, content, engagement, and conversion opportunity.

Figure 11.4

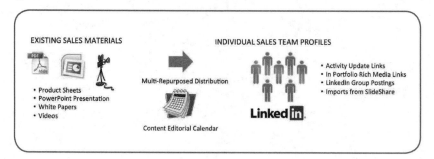

As you can see, the point of engagement with a customer prospect can work in favor of you and your sales team if you first listen and acknowledge the prospect's needs as they share in social conversations held in social communities. By knowing the customer's needs, you and your team can have a response plan that doesn't push your products, but rather, offers valuable tips and solutions your company can help enable. In social media environments, the selling dynamic is about attraction marketing.

The Value of the Email Signature

One of the most underutilized, yet most valuable touchpoints you can have is the email signature. Whether or not your company already has brand guidelines for email signatures, you may want to have links embedded in the signature template that give prospects the opportunity to review the LinkedIn profiles of you and your sales team. This gives the prospect an opportunity to assess the experience and qualifications of your sales team, and is a compelling reason to make sure your LinkedIn profiles reflect subject matter expertise, credentials, and customer testimonials that sell on your behalf.

Identify Key Metrics for Success

As a sales manager, you'll want to measure the success of the time you and your sales team spend on social media activities. The metrics for success can reflect key performance indicators (KPIs) you establish that can lead to the conversion funnel and ultimately to actual product or service sales. A simple way to assess the impact of your social media engagement efforts is to time-stamp social media activities and overlay that time period with any abnormal spikes you see in sales data or call center inquiries, for example, within that same timeframe. Achieve some early proof of concept in your social media sales and engagement efforts such as inbound call center volume, the number of likes or comments received by people to an activity update on LinkedIn, or engagement with a prospect on a social media network that lead to a request for proposal (RFP). These early results just might lead to getting more funding for your social media sales initiatives in next year's budget!

Understand the Customer Needs

One of the key benefits that social media brings to any strategic sales strategy is the ability to leverage real-time prospect insight through social listening. Simply stated, social listening is the ability to monitor social conversations that are happening across the social media platforms and web news sites. There are two key and free social listening tools you and your sales team can leverage to gain insight on target customer needs, and to identify when a prospect is looking for a solution. The following provides a brief description of each social listening tool and how best to use them.

Social Mention

Social Mention is a free social listening tool that provides a wealth of insight and is ideal to learn what people are saying about your brand, category, and company at large. You can gain the same insight about your competitors. One of the key insights is to learn how people emotively feel about a particular brand or company. This is called the sentiment score. You can conduct a search across all social media types, or narrow the search down (to blogs, for example).

Key insights around brand mentions include:

- **Strength:** The likelihood that your brand is being mentioned in social media. A simple calculation is used: phrase mentions within the last 24 hours divided by total possible mentions.

- **Passion:** Measures the likelihood of individuals talking about your brand repeatedly. For example, if you have a small group of very passionate advocates who talk about your products or brand all the time, you will have a higher Passion score. Conversely, if every brand mention is written by a different author, your brand will have a lower score. This measure can help you identify influential bloggers, for example, who advocate for your brand and who you will want to extend exclusive, first looks at your new products or services because they have a big social megaphone.

- **Reach:** Measures the range of brand influence. It is the number of unique authors referencing your brand divided by the total number of mentions.

- **Sentiment:** The ratio of mentions that are generally positive to those that are generally negative.

Advanced Twitter Search

Listening to all the activity on Twitter about your brand, category, or competitors can be valuable on multiple dimensions. Twitter Advanced Search delivers a wealth of insight and engagement opportunities to help drive your social selling strategy. Key to the advanced search features for Twitter are the filters you can set to conduct a highly targeted, niche search to determine:

- Who is tweeting about your brand? Identify potential brand advocates or dissenters that need to be engaged.

- What are they tweeting about? Evolve your selling points and capitalize on key features and benefits.

- Where are they tweeting? Improve alignment of your sales team in terms of geography, retail accounts, and so on.

- When are they tweeting? Use the opportunity for real time engagement when someone is online referencing your brand.

- Why are they tweeting? Is there insight to improve product and services or selling strategy positioning?

One of the best uses of Twitter Advanced Search is to filter only for tweets that ask a question regarding your brand, company, or product category. This could put you and your sales team at the right place at the right time to be a valued solution.

Mapping a Social Use Profile for Customer Prospects

Another key advantage of social listening is identifying where your customer prospects are already having conversations on social media. This insight gives you and your sales team the opportunity to align with where your customer prospects are, to engage them, and offer knowledge and solution value.

In addition to using social listening tools to identify where customer prospects are already having discussions, you and your sales team can set up Google Alerts to send email alerts when there are mentions of your brand, company, competitors, and product category. Building a database spreadsheet to log alerts and social listening insight leads to mapping the social use profile as described above.

Creating and Maintaining a Social Selling Content Strategy

Once you and your sales team have identified the issues of importance to your customer prospects, you can create a content strategy that keeps your sales team relevant, valued, and "on the radar" of social media networking communities. Central to this effort is organizing your content into primary segments:

- branded content created by your company (whitepapers, sales literature, and so on)
- industry content (trade journal articles)
- engagement content (asking questions, launching survey polls, and so on).

The following outlines the three primary content strategy segments and how they can be organized and distributed as part of your social selling strategy.

Branded Content

This is any content branded by your company. It could be product sell sheets, sales capabilities presentations, technical documents, whitepapers, or annual reports. When putting together an editorial calendar that plans the distribution of your branded content through social media channels, it may be advantageous to meet with your company's marketing team so you're in sync with the timing of your company's annual advertising, new product introductions, and promotions marketing calendar. Once you determine which content can be scheduled, plan with your sales team to make sure everyone is on the same calendar when distributing or posting content and company announcements across social media profiles.

Industry Content

Every content strategy deployed in social media should keep foremost in mind the importance of staying valued and relevant. This means that your content strategy should not be just about pushing your content and message, but being a reliable provider of non-branded content such as industry research trend reports, trade journal articles, and other sources of information that would be of value to your social network. The key is to strike a balance between distributing branded and nonbranded content that reflects the interest of you and your sales team and that puts the customer first. In the long run, the prospects in your social network will remember your value and just might become a customer.

A real benefit to maintaining a pipeline of content for distribution is the free tools available to find content of value and to schedule their distribution on social media sites. It's best to post content early in the morning on a weekday when people are most likely checking their email, reading news on the web, and checking out their social media networks before they start their work day. Again, it is best to mix up posting branded and nonbranded content that is highly relevant, valued, and can help your customer prospect solve a problem or make their day a little easier. It can also help support your sales teams' subject matter expertise and thought leadership—attributes that can attract and win over customer prospects. There are two free tools that can help you find and schedule the social media distribution of content:

- Feedly: This tool makes it easy to find and subscribe to industry-related newsfeeds, blogs, and articles. Feedly is a content aggregator that allows you to quickly scan your industry articles and either share them right away to LinkedIn, for example, or schedule them for distribution at a later time.

- Buffer: In the spirit of supporting a "stay on the radar" strategy on social media, the marriage of Feedly and Buffer work wonderfully together. You'll want to sign up for a free account at Buffer and set up a scheduling calendar of when you want industry-related content to be posted to your social media accounts.

You can also monitor how well your content is received by your social network (the number of likes, retweets, comments, and so on). This data is also handy to demonstrate that your content is being well received.

Engagement Content

Mixing your content strategy with approaches that proactively invite your customer prospect to engage is an effective way to show them that you care about their opinions and comments. Another key benefit of engagement content is the opportunity to gain current customer and market insight that can continuously be used to improve your selling points and sales value proposition. There are many types of engagement content for social media communities including surveys, polls, posting a question, sharing your tips, and so on. LinkedIn Groups, for example, provide opportunities for you and your sales team to actively engage members within an industry-specific group.

Engage Customer Prospects Based on Valued Relevance

As has been said a few times in this chapter, your customer prospects will measure the value you and your sales team bring to the social media community by what you contribute to the community, your usefulness, and timely ability to offer relevant solutions. In turn, you will want to make sure the time you and your sales team invest on social media is going toward engaging the right audience—not only potential customer prospects, but also potential referrals to prospects. The dynamics of social media brings into play the power of peer-to-peer influence and the purchasing decision chain. For example, a CFO can be highly influential on the purchasing decisions of the procurement manager. So you and your sales team will want to build and maintain social networks that include everyone in the buying decision, both direct buyers and influencers to the purchase. When building a quality social media network, it's key to keep focus on the fact that social media selling and marketing starts with building and earning trust relationships. It's not about connecting with companies, but rather, it's about connecting the people at your target customer accounts. LinkedIn, for example, offers many functions to build a relevant and quality social network through personal introductions, people you know who can introduce you to their contacts. Furthermore, you can use the advanced search function on LinkedIn with its filters that allow you to narrowly define your parameters to discover potential prospects based on company affiliation, title, and geography.

LinkedIn Groups—Be the Big Fish in a Small Pond

In addition to leveraging LinkedIn advanced search to build a quality social network, you and your sales team will want to join select LinkedIn groups. Instead of joining groups where there are a lot of service providers or suppliers that compete with you, think about participating in LinkedIn groups where you can own the voice in your area of expertise and service. In this way, you can engage with group discussions, launch engagement content strategies, and offer valuable content as a SME that can lead to potential sales conversion. Finally, one of the key advantages of joining select LinkedIn groups is the ability to connect with another member of that group as a first-degree connection, because you both belong to the same LinkedIn group.

Summing It Up

The objective of this chapter was to shine light on the fact that social media, and social media customer prospect engagement is fast becoming an essential part of an overall integrated sales strategy. Salespeople's time is precious, so it is important that the right amount of time be spent on it and that it is prioritized correctly. Leveraging social media as part of your overarching sales strategy can pay dividends if planned correctly. You will need solid LinkedIn profiles of your sales team that convey trust, credibility, and expertise. You will need a content strategy that first offers value to the social media community that ultimately places your products and services in a value context. And finally, you will need to build a social network anchored in human relationships where the presence and sincere contributions of you and your sales team can reflect well on your brand and ultimately help achieve your target quotas and make a positive impact on bottom line.

Action Plan

1. Activate social media listening, alerts, and advanced search on LinkedIn, Twitter, and Google to identify the most current engagement opportunities you can have with customers and prospects. Upgrade your company email signatures of your sales team—include links to your website and LinkedIn profiles. Is there an opportunity in the email signatures to add descriptive positioning of your brand differential or feature a call-to-action with a clickable link to featured content?

2. Do a LinkedIn profile analysis for your sales team. Does each individual profile include a consistent company description that aligns with marketing and branding? Are individual profiles effectively showing the breadth of experience and representing your sales team members as experts in your industry? Are you fully leveraging the exponential reach of your branded sales content to customer prospects by adding

links and sales information across all the LinkedIn profiles of your salespeople? Profiles do belong to the individual, but recommendations and suggestions can be made to strengthen. (You can be certain that prospects will check out your sales team members—know what your customer prospects are seeing.) Are there LinkedIn groups that your team or company should be proactively engaged with and where you can "own" the industry thought leadership voice?

3. Is the team ready for social media? Communications should include good grammar, spelling, and punctuation. (With exceptions like Twitter.) A certain writing skill should be present before encouraging your sales team members to go out and write in public. Give development options if they are needed, or see where there are opportunities to re-purpose messaging from the marketing department.

4. Identify which social media tools can be leveraged by your team. Check out tools like Social Mention if you don't already use them. Set up Google Alerts to monitor mentions of your company, your major competitors, and industry or product category at large. (Start with a few.)

5. Leverage the social media early adopters on your team. Share learning across the sales team.

6. Connect with marketing to see what they are doing in social media that can also help you and your sales team. For most companies, marketing drives the social media effort. Look for what your sales team can do in their respective sales territories to capitalize on your company's social media and content strategy efforts and adapt them for local markets and customer relevance.

References

http://socialmention.com

https://twitter.com/search-advanced

http://cloud.feedly.com

http://bufferapp.com

About the Author

Glenn Raines is the "revealer of value" at his consulting company, Social Media Moves, where he helps individuals and companies leverage emerging digital and social media strategies, tactics, and tools to achieve strategic organizational and personal career development goals. Glenn is nationally known for his thought leadership in developing LinkedIn and Google Profiles, and he authored the e-book, *Your Google Profile: Elevate Your Brand and Findability on the Web*. Glenn has recently developed social media thought leadership strategies for clients including the Royal Bank of Scotland and Bank of New York Mellon. Glenn also serves as a corporate trainer in digital and social media strategy where he helps companies and employees accelerate learning in the fast changing digital space. Recent training clients include global ad agencies Publicis Group and Omnicom Group. Currently Glenn is working with JP-Morgan Chase on developing their next generation corporate HR and organizational benefits global intranet.

12

Successfully Leading Virtual Teams

Renie McClay, MA, CPLP

Managing a remote team is different than managing a team that works together in the same building—but sales managers have known this for years. Managing a geographically dispersed sales team requires deliberate action and deliberate intention to make people feel like part of a larger team. For many of them, their sales team is the whole company because they don't often get a view of the larger picture. This chapter focuses on what it takes to build and sustain a successful virtual, or remote, team.

Virtual Team Tips

The Harvard Management Update recommends six steps to improve success in managing virtual teams. These are:

1. Create face time.

2. Set clear goals and expectations.

3. Make the work visible to the team.

4. Provide ongoing feedback.

5. Showcase team members' competence.

6. Foster cultural understanding on the team (Ross, 2006).

Building the Virtual Team

Two areas that can be challenging are developing a relationship with each team member and getting a group to function as a team. Both of these things are important to have a team that works together. This can be a challenge because distance can make connecting and building trust with each individual difficult. It is also important to help team members feel a connection to the larger organization. Let's look at these more closely.

An important part of building a sales team is to establish trust and build relationships among the team members. This takes deliberate time and effort to establish. As the sales team leader or manager, your behavior sets the tone and provides an example for the team. Be sure that you connect with each individual during occasional face-to-face meetings. Establish a schedule for team meetings and phone calls with individual reps to check in. Email can also be used to keep in touch, but should be used for less pressing issues or topics. Some best practice tips to help build a cohesive virtual team include:

- Be available. Access to managers is a huge issue for salespeople. Try to be available when they need you, if not, let them know when you will be, or provide an alternate way to reach you. Giving them whatever time you have left after all of your other responsibilities is not the right priority, nor is it setting a good example for the team.

- Demonstrate value. Show that each person is important and that you value him or her. Never talk badly about another team member.

- Make a plan and follow through. Good follow-through helps with efficiency and setting expectations.

- Collaborate. Help team members share their thoughts. Find reasons for the team to collaborate. This helps with getting to know each other and builds commitment to the team and trust.

- Connect to the larger group. Help team members connect with the larger organization. Sometimes their view of the entire company is Arizona. The manager is the key to providing the larger view.

- Assign a mentor. Mentors help team members feel a solid connection to the rest of the team and the organization.

- Improve your skills in managing conflict. Create an environment in which people are comfortable asking questions, speaking up, and asking for what they need.

- Get to know people. Prior to the start of your team meetings, take a few minutes for some "coffee talk." This can be an informal discussion on any non-work-related topic that interests the team. It's a great way for the team to get to know each other better. Encourage participation from all team members. Have each team member post a photo—something fun, from a recent vacation, a new baby or pet (on Pinterest or a Google Drive doc). Have everyone share something to stimulate the personal connection.

- Listen actively. Above all, be a good listener. Listen intently to hear what they are saying and what they mean.

- Vary media to keep in touch. Live conversations, face-to-face meetings, and phone calls are the best for building relationships. Webcams ramp up the personal connection of phone calls and are inexpensive. Emails are the worst for building relationships; it is great for sharing facts, quick reach-outs, and check-ins, but can lack context and be misunderstood. It is also helpful to navigate time zone differences. Consider the human interaction and bridge the geographical divide.

- Schedule face-to-face time. Face-to-face events build strong working relationships, help connect the team to the larger mission, and assist in career development and exposure. There is a cost for face-to-face meetings, but there is a potentially greater cost for not having them—turnover and disconnected, dissatisfied employees and customers.

- Leverage skills. Create a community between team members. Let others know who to contact for questions about which topic or highlight someone who has had recent success with something.

Another key ingredient to successfully managing virtual teams is recognizing a job well done on your team. Learn how individuals and the team prefer to be recognized. Ask them what is meaningful and then do what is impactful for them. Send gift cards to places people like, even if it is just coffee or lunch. A hand-written note recognizing achievement can make someone's day. "Good job" emails are fine, but have much less impact. When recognizing an achievement using the phone, make it a single purpose phone call.

Recognize Success

- State what they did well.
- Tell why this is important; what is the impact?
- Ask a question to get them talking about it.

If lunch is being served at a special meeting and someone is attending remotely, send them a gift card for a pizza or mail some food or snack they like so that they can share in this event virtually. You don't have to do this every time, but doing it once or twice and acknowledging the remote person leaves a lasting and positive impression.

If your primary responsibility is to develop and manage the team, then scheduling time with them should be a priority. As a result of attending a managing virtually class, a manager changed the way he scheduled his week.

Instead of scheduling his day with corporate meetings and commitments and then working in his team's needs, he first blocked time on his calendar for his team to reach him if they need to. He also started scheduling one-on-one calls weekly to stay caught up and offer assistance.

Onboarding New Salespeople

Hiring someone to be successful working in a virtual environment can be different than hiring someone to work in an office with their peers, easy access to their manager, and tech support. Hiring people who are goal-oriented, people-focused, good influencers, and good team players is key for any team. When hiring for geographically dispersed positions, it is also important to look for self-starters, good problem solvers, those who can ask for help when they need it, and individuals who are open to feedback. They should be independent, familiar with technology, and open to trying new things. Ideal candidates are also good, clear communicators.

Bringing someone new onto the team is particularly challenging in a virtual environment. How do you get to know that new employee? In-person time can speed up the process of getting to know each other and building trust. Here are some additional tips to consider whether you are meeting face-to-face or not:

- Plan a rock solid first week. That is when they will decide if they made the right choice coming to this company and choosing this job.
- Have a plan. Develop their training plans before they start. Don't put them in front of customers too soon, it could be embarrassing and will be a setback for the customer relationship.
- Be available. Be sensitive to the enormous amount of information they need to learn quickly.
- Stress open and honest communication. Encourage their zillions of questions. Give them opportunities to speak up and give their opinions.
- Lend visible support. Have a weekly check-in, at least for the first month. Find out what is going well and where support is needed.

- Communicate regularly. Do not rely too heavily on email. Use a variety of methods to stay in contact with your new team member.

- Ask questions. Figure out what motivates them.

- Share your expectations. Let them know what you expect during the training period and afterward.

- Provide "guard rails." Support them and help them to understand and be accepted in the culture of the organization.

- Assign a peer mentor. Help them gain the job knowledge and skills they need by providing someone they can go to for support.

- Make introductions. Make a personal introduction to the team, including a photo and personal interests. Help to make connections within the team.

- Remove barriers. Remember how hard it is to get answers when there is no one right down the hall to ask.

A new territory manager in a product training class had customers calling her with questions during her second week on the job. She said, "Not only do I not know the answer, I don't even understand the question." Make sure new hires are prepared for and comfortable with the industry and products before they take over accounts.

Managing Performance

Managing performance is different when you are not face-to-face. A sales manager managing an inside sales team will manage differently than a sales manager managing a remote team located in multiple states or on several continents. How do you know what and how your sales reps are doing? Here are some tips for managing a virtual sales team:

- Provide regular feedback that includes both positive and constructive comments. If possible, deliver feedback in person. Giving constructive feedback virtually is challenging, because both parties can miss nuances. Plan in advance what you are going to say and anticipate possible reactions, particularly when giving constructive feedback. Give feedback on an ongoing basis; don't save it up for performance reviews.

- Speak up. Let people know what you are noticing. Make it clear what you are picking up and discuss—don't just send an email about it.

- Articulate your expectations and communicate priorities. Verify that people know the priorities and can manage their time well.

- Make time for connection. One-on-ones are important. Seek them out. Talk to salespeople each week. Find out what is happening and what they are working on.

- Manage conflict. Conflict can be the single most challenging thing for many people. Create a safety zone, and encourage team members to speak up.

- Recognize and reward performance. Be sensitive to stressful times. Send random cards thanking individuals for their contributions.

- Have career discussions. If you don't want to lose them, let them know. Discuss where they want to go with the organization. If they are dissatisfied, by the time you find out, it is often too late to change things for the better.

- Manage to results. Share the important metrics and discuss them regularly. Give feedback on the results as well as the activities that will lead to results.

- Ask how you can help. If you aren't available when they need you, let them know when you will be available, or provide a back-up person or plan.

- Show care and compassion. Even if it isn't your strong suit, find a way.

- Celebrate success. This should be more than an email saying "nice job." Come up with a way to showcase success for the whole team to see.

- Pay attention. If underperformance is suspected, communicate clearly and often how things should be done and how they need to change. Talk to customers and co-workers to see what they are noticing.

- Make it their responsibility. Set it up so that your team members report their challenges and successes to you, rather than you having to reach out to them. It gives you more insights into what is going on for them and gives you additional information to talk to them about—reasons to talk and topics to connect on.

- Watch for silent periods. If they seem quiet or different than normal, reach out with a method other than email. See if all is well; be sensitive for a problem.

One of the issues with salespeople is that it is often hard for them to be visible to the organization. Help provide visibility for your team upward and across the organization. Stay connected to their major goals and ask about their progress. When success is achieved, share it with the team and copy other managers. Write down the company anniversary and birthday for each person and remember them.

How Do You Find Out What They Are Doing?

Simple. Ask great questions. Here are some for starters.

- What is going well?
- Are you facing any challenges? What are your ideas to handle them?
- What's going on you that are proud of?
- Tell me something good.
- What can I do for you?
- What can we do to take this to the next level?
- What is working so far? What seems not to be working?
- What have you noticed with…

These questions can help you monitor their activities and maintain a connection; it is not for the purpose of over-managing them. You want to reach out, not in a micro-managing way, but in a "what's up" or "need me for anything?" way.

Patrick Lencioni discusses the five building blocks for team functionality in *The Five Dysfunctions of a Team: A Leadership Fable*. This is a great book for leaders to read and for leadership teams to read and discuss. The five building blocks are trust, conflict, commitment, accountability, and results. Here are some quick and actionable ideas on how to do each, particularly when managing a virtual team.

Building Trust

- Admit when you are wrong.
- Have impeccable follow-through. If you miss something, apologize.
- Encourage teamwork.

- Build a team that supports each other; resist pitting them against each other.

- Be transparent, open, and honest with your intentions, when possible.

- Help to eliminate roadblocks.

- Communicate when you trust them to handle something.

- Show them you value their opinion.

- Ask for their feedback. Listen.

- Encourage their decision making.

- Support them and help them learn from mistakes.

Manage Conflict

- Don't get sucked into managing conflict using email. Pick up the phone. Encourage the team to do the same.

- Address opportunities quickly.

- Give people a chance to vent without penalty.

- Get face-to-face resolution where possible.

- Listen and strive to understand before you speak.

- Show respect to your team and show respect for their ideas.

- Work at identifying the underlying issue.

- Get their ideas for resolution; the manager doesn't have to have all the answers.

- Discuss possible solutions to help them understand and solve issues.

- Give a cool down period if helpful, but in general do not delay conversations.

- Follow up after an issue to ensure all is well.

- Realize your conflict management style and be sensitive to other's different styles.

Achieve Commitment

- Ensure role clarity.

- Keep goals top of mind.

- Let them figure out how to best get things done, when appropriate.
- Celebrate milestones, not just the achievement of the end goal.
- Recognize success both individually and in front of peers.
- Be transparent when you can to avoid feeling like you are checking up on them.
- Have honest and open communications where you can.
- Work to get group buy-in on appropriate topics.
- Use the CRM for appropriate dialogue—for positive reinforcement, not just to beat someone up.

Embrace Accountability

- Demonstrate owning results, mistakes, and successes.
- Evaluate performance fairly.
- Work toward clear and concise communication.
- Give frequent feedback, positive and constructive. Make it part of ongoing work, make it conversational.
- Communicate clear expectations, tell and show them what "good" looks like.
- Address poor performers. Lingering is bad for the whole team.
- Manage toward performance improvement.
- Share success stories.
- Get team members talking.

Focus on Results

- Demonstrate taking individual ownership.
- Set clear objectives and expectations.
- Recognize team results.
- Prioritize workload, tasks, and goals.
- Establish milestones.

Foster Cultural Understanding

What about the implications of managing global teams with people from different countries and cultures? The challenge for managers (and leaders) of multicultural teams is to build an atmosphere of camaraderie, mutual respect, effective communication, and productivity despite differing worldviews and physical environments. In essence, as a team leader or manager you must take a disparate group of people and cultures, and develop a team culture that is an amalgamation of the best of each of the cultures and strengths that the individual team members bring with them (Duarte and Snyder, 1999).

- When working with a person from a different country, use a resource like *When Cultures Collide* by Richard Lewis or *Gestures: The Dos and Taboos of Body Language Around the World* by Roger Axtell. There are valuable and helpful insights there that can help you to learn about the new culture.

- Stay open to ideas and solutions. A different culture may have a different approach that will work better for them.

- Tell people when you start managing them, "My intention is to be respectful of your culture."

- Be aware of direct versus indirect communication styles. If you are working with someone from a culture that prefers a more indirect communication style, start conversations gently and be sensitive when giving constructive feedback.

- If you are working with non-native speakers, allow extra time in one-on-one or group discussions. Watch jargon, sarcasm, and jokes. They will not be helpful in communicating your message (Irwin and McClay, 2008).

- Let people finish their thoughts. Know that some cultures will not interrupt or "fight for the mic," even if they have something important to add. Be aware yourself and make your team aware of these cultural aspects.

- Do not rely on email as your only communication method. Establish a relationship using webcams, webcasts, or phone calls. Using Skype is a cheap way to call with video.

- Don't avoid differences, showcase them. Help the team to understand the cultures of fellow team members. It can improve understanding and build trust.
- Rotate the time of meetings so everyone is inconvenienced equally. Establish black out time periods in order to have meetings at agreeable times. Keep a master holiday calendar.

For additional information on managing cultural differences, see the chapter in this book, "Managing Global Teams."

Global Teams Tip

Be attentive to non-native speakers who may not have a high comfort level with your language. Consider there could be a mix of comfort level in your audience, and that some people may need to hear what you've said, translate it, think of an answer, and translate the answer into your language. This is cause for pause!

Summing It Up

The stakes for managing virtual sales teams are high. Disengaged employees can cost the company a lot in terms of lack of productivity and customer satisfaction. Not being with employees in person may make it hard to pick up on an unhappy sales rep or customer. The loss can be significant in terms of sales quotas and profits missed, as well as in turnover costs of finding a replacement and having an open territory. The manager of a virtual team needs to provide the glue to fix the issues that lack of human contact can cause: lack of team spirit, trust, and productivity (McClay, 2009).

The solution is simple. A manager managing a virtual team has to be better than a manager who sees their people every day. You need to deliberately reach out for the things you would learn and see on the way to the coffee pot.

Action Plan

Do a quick check to see what you are doing to deliberately manage your team.

- What are you doing to make yourself available to your team?

- What are you doing to recognize and celebrate successes—both for the team and for individual team members?

- How do you connect new people with the team?

- Review the tips to help build a cohesive team. What will you incorporate into your meetings? Add it to your meeting agenda! What will you incorporate in ongoing communication with your team?

- In the section on Managing Performance, review the tips for managing a virtual sales team well. Choose two items you want to incorporate in your everyday managing of your people. Put them on sticky notes (either paper or electronic) as a reminder until they become habit.

Resources

Duarte, D., and N. Snyder, (1999). *Mastering Virtual Teams: Strategies, Tools, and Techniques That Succeed.* San Francisco: Jossey-Bass.

Irwin, L., and R. McClay, (2008). *The Essential Guide to Training Global Audiences.* San Francisco: Pfeiffer.

McClay, R. (2010). *Fortify Your Sales Force: Leading and Training Exceptional Teams.* San Francisco: Pfeiffer.

McClay, R. (2009). *10 Steps to Successful Teams.* Alexandra, VA: ASTD Press.

Ross, J. (2006). "Trust Makes the Team Go 'Round." *Harvard Management Update,* 11(6), 3–6. Retrieved from Business Source Complete Database.

About the Author

Renie McClay, MA, CPLP, has been successful in sales, management, and learning and performance roles at several Fortune 500 companies (Kraft, Pactiv, and Novartis). As founder of Inspired Learning LLC, she continues to bring her passion and practical approach to all project work. Inspired Learning LLC manages performance solutions, including design and delivery of energetic programs and projects around the world. She is the author of six books designed to improve effectiveness of teams, sales, and to add interaction and engagement to training for local and global audiences. She speaks at conferences like ASTD's International Conference & EXPO, SMT: Center for Sales Excellence, and regional ASTD Chapter conferences. She has been invited to facilitate workshops for audiences in North America, Europe, Africa, Latin America, Asia, and Australia—both in person and virtually. She is a certified online instructor and facilitates online and in person for Roosevelt University and Concordia University. She is an honoree for the International Business Awards and The Stevie Awards for Women. She is a Certified Professional of Learning and Performance (CPLP) and has a master's degree in global talent development from DePaul University.

Appendix
Sales Manager Skills Assessment

Ken Phillips

Knowing your current strengths and development needs is the first step to improving your job performance. However, unless you are one of the fortunate few who receive regular, ongoing feedback about your job performance, you likely only have a vague idea about what things you are doing well and what you need to improve.

One proven method for gaining this insight is to honestly complete a self-assessment about your own job behavior or performance. I say honestly because if you complete a self-assessment with the intent of making yourself look better or worse than you really are, the results will not help you improve.

The Sales Manager Skills Assessment is designed to provide you with specific information regarding your strengths and development needs as a sales manager. The value of this information is that it will provide you with a focus for improving your future performance and serve as reinforcement for the things you are already doing well.

The assessment consists of 18 statements divided into three dimensions. Taken from the ASTD World-Class Sales Competency Model·these dimensions represent Areas of Expertise (AOEs) that were rated as having high importance for sales managers during a research study that created the model. A brief description of each scale follows:

- **Setting Sales Strategy:** Helps an organization expand its understanding of professional selling and continuously improve sales performance by advancing innovative sales practices and sales team configuration strategies; promotes integrated sales automation tools and processes; and establishes interface processes and working relationships with key business executives (for example, marketing, engineering, supply chain, and so on).

- **Managing Within the Sales Ecosystem:** Monitors individual sales rep and sales team metrics achievement (for example, progress against goal, quota performance, sales funnel activity, margin, and so forth); determines functional or organizational structure (territory alignment, team organization, and so on); conducts recruitment, hiring, promotion, performance appraisal, career development, and termination; manages individual sales rep and sales team expectations and responsibilities; and works with peers and upper management to optimally align workload and allocate resources.

- **Coaching for Sales Results:** Draws out, develops, and hones the best performance of individual sales reps and sales teams by providing on-the-job reinforcement and corrective feedback to maximize strengths and identify development needs; models appropriate and expected behavior; and ensures that each sales rep's performance is linked to sales results.

In addition to identifying Areas of Expertise, the research study also identified a series of key actions associated with each AOE. The key actions represent critical behaviors and activities sales managers must perform in each AOE in order to carry out their role effectively, and form the basis for the 18 behavioral statements that comprise the Sales Manager Skills Assessment. Specific instructions for completing the assessment are located with the inventory along with a scoring form, scoring interpretation information, and an action planning activity.

Sales Manager Skills Assessment
Instructions

- The assessment consists of 18 statements, which describe behaviors identified as important for sales managers to engage in while performing their job.

- Carefully read the first statement. Keeping in mind your own approach to performing your role as sales manager, indicate how often you engage in the behavior along a continuum from Never (1) to Always (7).

- Circle the number that corresponds to your choice for each statement. You must make a choice for all 18 statements in order for the assessment to be scored accurately.

- Make your choices based on how you actually behave, not on how you think you should behave.

Table A.1

	Statement	Never						Always
1.	I look for themes and obstacles that may adversely affect my sales reps' effectiveness and then introduce new strategies and sales practices to mitigate them.	1	2	3	4	5	6	7
2.	I set priorities and expectations to ensure that all my sales reps' selling activities are aligned with corporate strategies and goals.	1	2	3	4	5	6	7
3.	During joint sales calls, I assume the role of observer and look to identify patterns of behavior that illustrate the sales rep's strengths and development needs.	1	2	3	4	5	6	7
4.	I create a strategic plan to guide the sales activities in my area, ensure that it aligns with the plans developed by other sales managers, and make adjustments as needed.	1	2	3	4	5	6	7

	Statement	Never						Always
5.	I establish an operating budget and track sales rep spending and sales discounts to ensure appropriate margins are maintained.	1	2	3	4	5	6	7
6.	When providing feedback to a sales rep, I maintain a balance between positive and corrective feedback.	1	2	3	4	5	6	7
7.	I build alliances with other people in the company (product development, marketing, and supply chain managers, and so on) who can help my sales reps achieve their sales goals.	1	2	3	4	5	6	7
8.	I ensure that my sales reps target their calling efforts on high priority accounts that align with company strategy.	1	2	3	4	5	6	7
9.	When working with an individual sales rep or my sales team, I try to discover what motivates them and then look for ways to align them with organizational goals.	1	2	3	4	5	6	7
10.	I use a variety of communication channels (email, texting, phone calls, and face-to-face meetings) to keep my sales reps motivated and focused on their sales strategies.	1	2	3	4	5	6	7
11.	I serve as a filter and screen disruptions that might cause my sales reps to lose focus on their selling activities.	1	2	3	4	5	6	7
12.	I ensure that all my sales reps understand how their individual performance aligns to the organization's strategic initiatives and goals.	1	2	3	4	5	6	7
13.	When appropriate, I reconfigure my sales reps' territories in order to improve overall sales effectiveness.	1	2	3	4	5	6	7

	Statement	Never						Always
14.	I conduct check-ins and hold meetings with my sales reps to ensure they are on track to hit their established sales plans.	1	2	3	4	5	6	7
15.	When appropriate, I model the company's desired sales techniques and best practices so that my sales reps can learn from my example.	1	2	3	4	5	6	7
16.	I establish hiring criteria, review candidate qualifications, provide input into the selection process, and facilitate the onboarding of new hires.	1	2	3	4	5	6	7
17.	I provide my sales reps with regular opportunities to enhance their sales skills and knowledge though techniques such as coaching, mentoring, job sharing, and training.	1	2	3	4	5	6	7
18.	I use rewards and recognition to drive sales performance at both the individual sales rep and team level.	1	2	3	4	5	6	7

Your Behavior Scores
Instructions

- The three AOEs identified as having high importance for sales managers are listed in Table A.2. Each number in the second column represents a statement from the assessment (Table A.1).

- Refer to the table on the next page to calculate your score for each AOE in Table A.3. Replace each statement number with your score for that question.

- Total the numerical values on each dimension in order to obtain a score for each one.

- After finding your score on each dimension, total all three scores to determine your overall score.

Table A.2

AOE	Statements	Score
Setting Sales Strategy	1 + 4 + 7 + 10 + 13 =	
Managing Within the Sales Ecosystem	2 + 5 + 8 + 11 + 14 + 16 + 18 =	
Coaching for Sales Results	3 + 6 + 9 + 12 + 15 + 17 =	
Add your scores on each dimension to get your overall score:		

Table A.3

AOE	Statements	Score
Setting Sales Strategy		
Managing Within the Sales Ecosystem		
Coaching for Sales Results		
Add your scores on each dimension to get your overall score:		

What Your Scores Mean

The Sales Manager Skills Assessment is designed to assess your use of the critical behaviors and key activities that sales managers must perform in order to carry out their role effectively.

Your overall score provides you with a general picture of how frequently you perform the critical behaviors and key activities associated with each of the three AOEs. This score will range between 126 (frequent use of the critical behaviors and key activities) and 18 (little to no use of the critical behaviors and key activities).

Your three dimension scores indicate how often you use the specific critical behaviors and activities associated with each dimension. Scores on each will range between 35 (frequent use) and 5 (no use) for Setting Sales Strategy, between 49 (frequent use) and 7 (no use) for Managing Within the Sales Ecosystem, and between 42 (frequent use) and 6 (no use) for Coaching for Sales Results.

The Score Ranges chart on the next page will help you interpret your overall and dimension scores more accurately. The chart categorizes all scores into the ranges of "Strong," "Competent," and "Needs Development." Locate your scores on the chart and circle the range of numbers within which each of your scores fall. The overall column of the chart will help you better interpret your overall use of the critical behaviors and activities sales managers must perform in order to carry out their role effectively. The AOE columns of the chart are designed to help you gain more specific insight into your strengths and development needs in each of the three areas.

Take a moment to notice whether your scores fall above or below competent. If you have scores that fall into the strong category either overall or in any of the three AOEs, congratulations! These scores show that you use the behaviors and activities in these areas more than average.

On the other hand, if you have scores in either the competent or needs development categories, these identify areas where there is room for improvement, with scores in the needs development category having the highest priority.

Table A.4: Score Ranges Chart

	Setting Sales Strategy	Managing Within Sales Ecosystem	Coaching for Sales Results	Overall
Strong	28-35	39-49	34-42	101-126
Competent	19-34	27-38	23-33	69-100
Needs Development	5-18	7-26	6-22	18-68

Instructions

- Refer back to the Score Ranges Chart.
- Note your highest and lowest scores.
- Think about your role as sales manager and the duties and activities you perform and answer the following questions.

1. What are your overall reactions to your scores?

_____

_____

_____

_____

2. Which results pleased you the most?

_____

_____

_____

3. What scores, if any, surprised you?

_____

_____

_____

4. What steps can you take to improve your scores?

_____

_____

_____

_____

5. What obstacles might keep you from taking the steps listed above and how can you overcome them?

_____

_____

_____

_____

About the Author

Ken is founder and CEO of Phillips Associates, a consulting and publishing company with expertise in measurement and evaluation of learning, performance management, and sales performance. He has more than 30 years of experience designing learning instruments and assessments and has authored more than a dozen published learning instruments. He regularly speaks to American Society for Training & Development (ASTD) groups and university classes, including the ASTD International Conference & EXPO. Prior to pursuing a Ph.D. in the combined fields of organization behavior and educational administration at Northwestern University, Ken held management positions with two colleges and two national corporations.